The Healthaliciously Good Cookbook
By Aurélie Paré

Published by Aurelie's Healthy Cuisine

Printed in Canada

Graphic Design by Nadine Cormier
Illustrations by Claire Langlois
Editing by Colleen Landry
Photography by Aurélie Paré

About Nutritional Information

All of the nutritional information in this book is provided by www.NutritionData.com. All the information, while thought to be true, is not guaranteed and is intended only to give the reader a rough estimate of the nutritive value of any given recipe.

Calories, total fat (fat), sodium*, carbohydrates, fiber, sugar, protein, and omega 3 fatty acids (Omega 3) are always listed, but vitamin A (VA), vitamin C (VC), vitamin D (VD), vitamin E (VE), vitamin K (VK), thiamin, riboflavin, niacin, vitamin B6 (B6), folate, vitamin B12 (B12), vitamin B5 (B5), calcium, iron, magnesium, phosphorus, potassium, zinc, copper, manganese, and selenium are only listed if one serving has 2% or more of that vitamin or mineral. Percentages are based on Recommended Daily Values.

* Amounts of sodium are not included in soup recipes as the amount of sodium in vegetable broth can vary widely.

Table of Contents

A Big Thank You

to all the people who helped make this cookbook possible....

Claire Langlois (my mother) who not only drew the beautiful illustrations for this cookbook, but also helped in a countless number (truly) of ways to make this book possible.

Nadine Cormier who generously created the gorgeous graphic design layout for this cookbook as well as the front cover design and in addition gave support and encouragement.

Colleen Landry who carefully revised, checked, and edited the cookbook manuscript and tested a few recipes to boot.

Jean-Louis Paré (my father) who helped on a technological level as well as with the building of the aurelieshealthycuisine.com website.

Frederik Paré (my younger brother) who fabricated the ceramic bowl pictured on the front cover.

My family who endured plenty of recipe testing and lots of cookbook chaos.

And of course, to Everyone who gave their opinions, suggestions, and encouragement...

May you all enjoy this book very much and savor numerous delicious dishes.

Introduction

My love of cooking can be traced back to when I was eleven and my mother put me in charge of making supper once a week, a question of learning to appreciate the effort put into home cooked meals. I quickly put myself to the task of learning the basics of cooking- learning how to cook simple things such as pasta (my favorite food) and steamed veggies and learning how to follow recipes.

I wasn't initially interested in healthy cooking. It was about a year after I started to cook, when I became interested in vegetarianism and nutrition, that I started thinking about healthy cooking. At this point, I learned to concoct healthy meals and to prepare healthy foods.

With time, just making existing healthy recipes didn't clinch it for me. I began to think of all the possibilities that healthy cooking could offer- so many of them unexplored and unknown- and ran to the kitchen to experiment. My early experiments in the kitchen weren't always successful, but I didn't give up. I built up a collection of recipes, a mixture of "health-a-fied" old favorites and unique, new recipes, all of which met my strict standards for health, taste, and convenience. From this point on, I became obsessed with sharing these recipes with the world in order to prove that healthy cooking could be rewarding, practical, and fun. In order to do that, I wrote *The Healthaliciously Good Cookbook* and founded Aurelie's Healthy Cuisine, a company dedicated to showing people how to cook healthily and tastily.

In this book, I offer you the recipes that started it all (or rather their shaped-up and revised descendents) and the sincere hope that you will enjoy them and treasure them for years to come. The recipes that I share with you here are my family's favorites, the ones that grace our table over and over again. Most of them can be prepared in less than 45 minutes and use ingredients or offer options for ingredients that you can easily find at your local grocery store. They are (of course) very healthy, being made with whole grains, legumes, fruits, nuts, and vegetables- foods that the Canadian and American food guides recommend eating more of. Healthy food seems to have been forgotten in today's society, which is unfortunate, since healthy food helps prevent disease and obesity (wide spread problems in today's world) and gives us energy and vitality.

So what are you waiting for? Go to the kitchen, make a recipe, and reap the benefits of eating and cooking healthaliciously!

Kitchen Equipment and Tools

A variety of kitchen equipment and tools are needed to prepare the recipes throughout this book. Below, I've included a few lists which enumerate the tools you'll need.

Preparatory Tools

I like to call the tools that help you prepare the ingredients for a recipe "preparatory" tools as they help "prepare" food. Here is a list of preparatory tools to have on hand:

- **Citrus juicer**
- **Cutting board**
- **Garlic press**
- **Measuring cups**
- **Measuring spoons**
- **Vegetable peeler**
- **Vegetable grater**
  (or food processor with shredding setting)

Kitchen Knives

There is said to be 3 knives that are absolutely necessary in every kitchen: the chef's knife, the paring knife, and the serrated knife. The chef's knife is the all-purpose knife used for vegetable and herb chopping. Its blade is typically 6 to 10 inches long and is typically wider than other knives. The paring knife is the "baby" chef knife that's only 2 to 4 inches long. It is used for all the small jobs that you can't do with a chef's knife. The serrated knife has a jagged blade and is used for cutting textured food such as bread. Although only one serrated knife is usually recommended, I suggest having two: a larger one and a smaller one. This way, you'll have greater ease with all the jobs that require serrated knives, not just the big ones.

* **Remember to use caution while using knives** and to keep them away from small children. Administer proper care to your knives to make them last. Drying them immediately after washing and keeping them regularly sharpened will keep them in tip-top shape and may even help to prevent accidents.

Kitchen Equipment and Tools: symbols

If you flip through the pages of this book, you will no doubt notice the symbols in the top right-hand corners of each page that indicate which equipment and tools (preparatory tools excluded) will be used in a recipe. In addition, each recipe mentions which tools you will need in the recipe directions.

Listed below is the key for decoding the kitchen equipment and tool symbols:

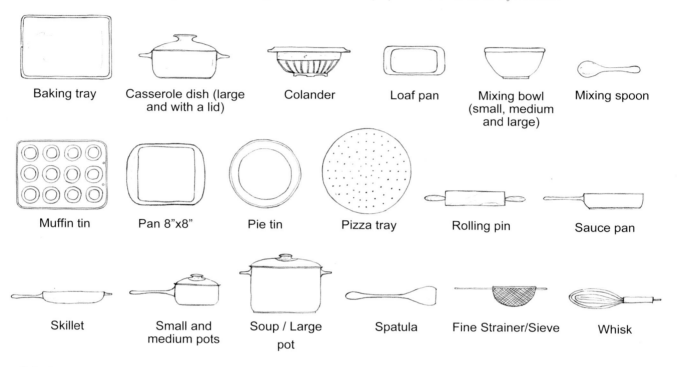

Baking tray	Casserole dish (large and with a lid)	Colander
Loaf pan	Mixing bowl (small, medium and large)	Mixing spoon

Muffin tin   Pan 8"x8"   Pie tin   Pizza tray   Rolling pin   Sauce pan

Skillet   Small and medium pots   Soup / Large pot   Spatula   Fine Strainer/Sieve   Whisk

Grinder

A small, electronic, coffee grinder is needed for many recipes in which you need to grind nuts or oats into flour/ paste. Since I never call for making a very fine flour or grinding anything harder than a coffee bean using a grinder, an inexpensive model (grinders are usually 12 dollars at their cheapest) will work just as well as a more expensive model when used to make one of my recipes.

Handheld Blender

At our house, the handheld blender rules the kitchen where we make good use of it on a daily basis. I prefer a handheld blender to a blender or food processor as it allows me to have more hands-on control with the blending and is easier to clean up as I can blend directly in the mixing bowl instead of having to transfer everything to a bulky blender. Although you can pick up a handheld blender for as little as 12 dollars, it's preferable to splurge a bit on this item and buy a better quality machine that will last longer and do its job well. That being said, pricey items are not always good quality, so use reviews and recommendations to figure out which handheld blender is best for you.

* **A note of caution:** Do not attempt heavy duty jobs with a handheld blender (Example: Pureeing nuts into nut butter or blending whole, raw vegetables such as carrots into a puree.) as there is a risk of electrical shock and it may burn the motor out.

Healthy Ingredients

At the base of every healthy meal and of every healthy diet, there are healthy foods and ingredients. Healthy foods and ingredients could be defined as foods that provide a good blend of nutrients in relativity to the amount of the food and its use. Healthy foods can be divided into 4 basic categories: whole grains, legumes, nuts, and fruits and vegetables. These types of foods can serve as building blocks for healthy recipes. When well-prepared and handled, these foods can be tasty, delicious, and convenient.

Choosing Healthy Foods: organics and locally grown foods

In recent years, we've been hearing more and more about organic and locally grown foods. Organic foods are foods that are grown without pesticides and that are not genetically modified, but may be more expensive as more labor is required to produce organic foods than conventional foods. Locally grown foods are foods that are grown in a close proximity to one's home and tend to be less expensive as consumers are not paying for the transportation of the food. Organic food is touted as being good for the environment, higher in nutrients, free of harmful pesticides, and tastier when compared to conventionally grown foods. Local foods are touted as being higher in nutrients and better for the environment because they are not shipped from distant lands. Ideally, it is best to eat foods that are both organic and local. In many towns and cities, organic and local produce can be obtained at weekly farmer's markets, where farmers get together in one common place to sell their crops.

Storing and preparing foods

Grains and legumes

Store uncooked grains and legumes in glass jars* in cool dry places for up to a year (after this nutritional value may decrease). Prepare them according to the grain and legume cooking charts on pages 11 and 10.

Seeds, nuts, and flour

Store these foods in glass jars* in the refrigerator. Nut and seed butters as well as wheat germ should be stored this way.

Oils and yeast

Store oils in dark-colored glass jars for 4 to 6 months. If oil begins to taste bitter, discard it. A bitter taste indicates rancid oil. Active dry yeast should be stored in the same conditions as oil, although in a cooler place.

Spices, dried herbs, and nutritional yeast

Store In cool, dry places devoid of light and humidity.

Salt, baking soda, and baking powder

Store in dry, cool places.

Store in airtight containers in the refrigerator.

Different vegetables and fruits should be stored different ways:

- Apples, bananas, citrus fruit, potatoes, garlic, and onions should be stored at room temperature.

- Certain fruits and vegetables should be stored at room temperature until ripe. If they are not eaten immediately after becoming ripe, they can be stored in the refrigerator. These include tomatoes, plums, peaches, melons, and avocados

- Other fruits such as berries and grapes should be stored in the refrigerator immediately, but should be eaten as soon as possible after this.

- Crisp and crunchy vegetables should be stored in a crisper in opened plastic bags. Plastic towels can be placed in the bottom of the crisper to absorb moisture. Note: The green leafy tops of root vegetables (such as carrots) should be cut off before storage as they drain vegetables of moisture.

- Mushrooms should be stored in a paper bag in the refrigerator. They should not be soaked in water when washed.

Before cooking or eating vegetables and fruits, let them soak in a mixture of vinegar and water for a few minutes and then rinse them well with water. If necessary, scrub them down with a bit of baking soda to clean them.

Leftovers can be frozen in single servings and then stored in airtight containers in the refrigerator. Reheat them in a toaster oven or on the stove.

Baked goods, while best the day of, can be stored in cookie tins wrapped tightly with plastic wrap for up to three days. Freeze baked goods by wrapping cooled baked goods first in plastic wrap, then in wax paper, and lastly in aluminium foil. Store them in an airtight container in the freezer for up to a few weeks. To thaw, heat the unwrapped bake goods in a 300 degree oven and serve immediately.

✳ I reuse empty marinara jars as storage containers. To prepare marinara jars for reuse, make sure to wash them thoroughly with soap and water. Remove any labels by letting hot water run onto them to ease peeling. To remove the label glue, use steel wool. Remove tomato stains from the lids by letting them sit in the sun for a day. Finally, sterilize the jars. Bake the jars (open, not sealed) in an oven preheated to 170º F for 5 minutes. Remove from oven, let cool, and then fill with food.

Cooking Charts

Cooking Grains and Legumes
Legume Chart

Legume (1 cup dry)	Amount of soaking time	Amount of cooking water	Amount of cooking time	Amount Yield
Black Beans	Overnight	4 cups	1 hour to 1 1/2 hour	About 2 cups
Black-eyed Peas	Overnight	3 cups	1 hour	About 2 cups
Chickpeas	Overnight	4 cups	1 to 3 hours	About 2 cups
Kidney beans	Overnight	3 cups	1 hour	About 2 cups
Lentils (Green)	None	2 cups	1/2 hour to 1 hour	About 2 cups
Lentils (Red)	None	3 cups	1/2 hour	About 2 1/2 cups
Pinto Beans	Overnight	3 cups	1 1/2 hour	About 2 1/2 cups
Split Peas (Yellow)	None	4 cups	1 1/2 hour	About 2 cups

The table above shows you cooking information for all the types of beans used in this book. Remember that all values are approximate. To prepare dried beans, rinse and drain them, discarding malformed beans. Place the beans in a large bowl and cover them with about 4 inches of water. Let soak overnight. (Skip this step if soaking is not required.) In the morning, drain and rinse the beans. Transfer the beans to a large pot and add cooking water and salt (if desired). Bring the water to a boil and then let it simmer for cooking time directed above or until beans are tender. Drain and rinse once more (If you wish, you can reserve the bean cooking water to make vegetable broth on p. 19.). Use the beans immediately or store them in the refrigerator. Cooked beans will stay good for about 4 days in the refrigerator. They can also be frozen in airtight containers in the freezer, where they will keep for up to a month. Thaw them in the refrigerator before using.

Fresh Beans

While dried beans are certainly easier to find, if you're lucky enough to find fresh beans (and that is lucky- fresh beans have a great, fresh flavor and take very little time to cook) here's how to cook them. Half-fill a large pot with water and bring the water to a boil. Add shelled beans and simmer for about 10 minutes or until tender. Drain and rinse the beans, use them immediately or store them in the refrigerator.

✳ Digestive Problems

Many people fear having flatulence or discomfort after eating beans. The easiest way to avoid this is to soak and cook the beans thoroughly and to eat small portions of beans to begin with and gradually increase them in size.

Grain Cooking Chart

Grain (1 cup dry)	Amount of cooking water	Cooking Method	Amount of cooking time	Amount Yield
Barley (hulled)	3 cups	Traditional method	Slightly over an hour	3 1/2 cups
Couscous (whole wheat)	1 cup	Bring water to a boil. Take off heat, stir in couscous, let sit until all water is absorbed	5 to 10 minutes	2 cups
Rolled oats	2 1/2 cups	Traditional method	5 minutes	3 cups
Millet	2 cups	Traditional method	20 minutes	3 cups
Brown Rice	2 cups	Traditional method	20 minutes	3 cups
Quinoa	2 cups	Quinoa has natural "insect repellent" on it that will give it a bitter flavor if not washed off. Soak quinoa in a bowl of water for 20 minutes, drain, and rinse. Use Traditional Method to cook.	About 35 minutes (includes soaking)	3 cups

Traditional Method

I call this the "traditional" method since so many grains are cooked this way. Rinse and drain the grains, discarding any malformed grains. Mix grains in a medium-sized pot with cooking water and bring to a boil. Stir and reduce to low, cover, and let simmer until grains are cooked. Once cooked, set aside for about 5 minutes. Afterwards, fluff the grains with a fork. Use immediately in recipes, as a side dish, or refrigerate for later use. Most grains will stay good for a few days when refrigerated.

✳ If planning to serve cooked grains as a simple side dish, vegetable broth can be used instead of water and herbs and spices can be added to make more flavorful grains.

Spices and Herbs

Spices and herbs are wonderful, flavorful additions to healthy dishes. Below is a list of herbs and spices used throughout this book.

- **Basil (dried)**
- **Bay leaf (dried)**
- **Black pepper**
- **Cardamom (ground)**
- **Cayenne pepper**
- **Celery seed**
- **Chili powder**
- **Cilantro (dried)**
- **Cinnamon (ground)**
- **Cloves**
- **Cumin**
- **Dill (dried)**
- **Fennel seed**
- **Garlic powder**
- **Ginger (dried and fresh)**
- **Nutmeg**
- **Onion powder**
- **Oregano (dried)**
- **Paprika**
- **Parsley (dried and fresh)**
- **Rosemary (dried)**
- **Sage (dried)**
- **Savory (dried)**
- **Seasoning salt**
- **Salt**
- **Thyme (dried)**

Seasoning Mixes

In addition to plain spices and herbs, I use seasoning mixes made with a variety of spices and herbs. The following are the mixes used throughout this book:

Curry powder

Curry powder is a blend of Indian spices typically used to season curries, but can also be used to give a curry flavor to a wide variety of dishes. This is a spice mix I recommend buying instead of making as it is widely available and curry powder can contain up to 30 different spices!

Garam Masala

Garam Masala is an Indian spice mix that can be used to season Indian dishes. I don't use this seasoning very often, only once (in Indian Spiced Quinoa Rolls on p. 60) so only buy it if you are planning on preparing this recipe. I recommend buying Garam Masala over making it as a few unusual spices and herbs are needed to make it.

Italian seasoning

Italian seasoning is an all-purpose seasoning that can be used not only in Italian dishes, but in many other dishes as well. You can buy this seasoning or make it yourself by mixing equal parts thyme, oregano, basil, sage, marjoram, rosemary, and savory.

Montreal steak spice seasoning

Despite its name, this salty and spicy seasoning is not just for steak. It can add flavor to bean burgers and sauces as well. You can buy this seasoning or make it yourself, by combining 6 parts salt to 2 parts red pepper flakes, ground coriander seeds, black pepper, paprika, dill weed, onion powder, and garlic powder.

Pumpkin pie spice

Not just for pies, this seasoning adds spice to granola and baked goods and can replace cinnamon in some recipes. You can buy this seasoning or make it yourself, by combining 1 part nutmeg (or half nutmeg and half cloves) ginger, and allspice to 2 parts cinnamon.

Fresh Herbs

Aside from fresh parsley and fresh ginger, I do not call for fresh spices/herbs in my recipes as they are not widely available year-round and can be expensive when available unless they are garden fresh. However, fresh herbs are definitely preferable to dried herbs, so if fresh herbs are available to you, substitute 1 tbsp finely minced fresh herb for 1 tsp dried herb.

Frozen Herbs vs. Dried Herbs

Although none of my recipes call for frozen herbs, I do wish to discuss the topic. While dried herbs may be more convenient and all-purpose, frozen herbs retain more of the fresh herb's original flavor and can be used in soups and sauces. If you want, you can replace 1 tsp dried herb with 1 tbsp fresh herb in frozen form in soup and sauce recipes. To make your own frozen herbs, place 1 tbsp finely minced fresh herb in an ice cube mold and fill with just enough water or vegetable broth to fill the mold. Freeze until solid, then remove the cubes from the mold, and transfer to a plastic freezer bag or airtight container. Keep frozen until needed. To add to a recipe, simply stir a frozen cube of herb into a warm sauce or soup.

Glossary of Ingredients

Although most of the ingredients in this book are pretty basic, I sometimes call for ingredients that aren't very well known or that may be a bit harder to prepare than others. In this glossary of ingredients, you can learn where to get these ingredients, how to prepare them, and other pertinent information.

* Most of these ingredients can be found at grocery stores/supermarkets (depending on where you live) but some may only be available at health/bulk food stores in which case it is recommended that you buy these foods in large quantities if you are planning to use them frequently. Keep in mind that many of these ingredients may not be kept in the same place on the shelves from one grocery store to another, so ask store employees to help you locate the ingredients you need.

Looking for almond butter? See nut/seed butter.

Alternative milk

Alternative milks include almond, rice, and soy milks among others. Look for the fortified types as they are a more appropriate substitute for dairy milk than the ones that are not. They can be used in most recipes in which dairy milk is used. Keep in mind, however that rice milks (especially) and other milks tend to be sweeter than dairy milk and may not be suitable for savory dishes. Rice and almond milk are available in most grocery/super stores in aseptic containers as well as in cartons. Make sure to use unsweetened or regular fortified varieties in the recipes in this book unless otherwise instructed.

Apple juice concentrate

I use apple juice concentrate (sold in the freezer section of a grocery store) as a sweetener in many of my recipes as an alternative to sugar. Why apple juice instead of honey, maple syrup, agave nectar, or demera sugar? It is less expensive and more widely available, making it a convenient sweetener for most people. Desserts made with fruit juice will be a bit less sweet than some high-sugar desserts however, so if you are used to eating a lot of sugar, slowly transition to using fruit juice by using half juice and half maple syrup (which tastes sweeter) instead of all juice or by dissolving brown sugar into the juice. You may need to add a bit more liquid to the recipe if you don't use all apple juice concentrate however, so adjust the amount of liquid ingredients accordingly. As a rule of thumb, 1 can of juice is equivalent to 1 2/3 cup juice. Make sure to measure out the juice while it is still frozen (slush consistency).

Looking for breadcrumbs? See Whole Grain Bread.

Butternut Squash

Butternut Squash is a winter squash similar to pumpkin in taste. It has a smooth, oblong shape and a beige exterior. Its inside is a yellow-orange color. It has a taste and texture perfect for soups and sauces. To cook it (which you will have to do before using it in a recipe), follow the directions below.

* **DIY: Cooked Butternut Squash**
To cook a butternut squash, cut the squash in half lengthwise, scoop out the seeds with a spoon, place the squash cut-side down on an oiled baking tray, and bake it at 375° F for about an hour or until fork tender.

Carob Powder/Chips

Carob is very similar to chocolate in taste and appearance but it offers more nutrients than chocolate and is caffeine-free, making it less guilt-provoking than its look-a-like. In this cookbook, it is used in the form of carob chips and carob powder, both of which can be found at health food stores and bulk food stores. Make sure to choose varieties free of unhealthy hydrogenated oils.

Looking for cashew butter? See nut/seed butter.

Looking for chickpeas? See Legumes.

Coconut Milk

A rich milk made from coconut, coconut milk adds finger-licking goodness to recipes. It is available at most grocery stores in the ethnic food section. Make sure to use regular coconut milk and not light coconut milk or coconut cream. Remember to shake the can well before opening it as coconut milk tends to separate. Gradually add coconut milk to recipes; the thickness of the milk can vary from one brand to another and you may need to adjust the amount of liquid slightly after adding the coconut milk.

Looking for croutons? See Whole Grain Bread.

Looking for date puree? See Dried Fruit Purees.

Dried Fruit Puree

Dried fruit purees are exactly what they sound like- purees made from dried fruit. They act as a sweetener and add fruity flavor to dishes. In this book, date and apricot purees are called for. Since you can't find dried fruit purees in stores, you will need to make your own according to the directions below.

* **DIY: Dried Fruit Puree**
   To make dried fruit puree, simmer about a cup of dried fruit of choice with a few tablespoons of water in a small pot until the dried fruit is very soft and no water is left (alternatively, soak overnight covered in water, then drain water). Using a handheld blender, puree dried fruit until smooth. Makes 1/2 cup. Will keep in the refrigerator for about a week.

Flax

Flaxseeds are small, shiny, and nutritious seeds that are a good source of omega 3 fatty acids, which are important, healthy fats. The possibilities are endless when it comes to incorporating this nutrition powerhouse into your diet. Throughout this book, I suggest places where flax meal or oil can be added. Remember to always store flax meal and oil in the refrigerator and never to heat flax oil, doing otherwise will destroy their delicate fatty acids. Note: It's preferable to eat flax meal (ground flaxseeds) rather than whole flaxseeds since you will absorb the omega 3s better.

Flour

Throughout this book, I use a variety of flours. Here is a list of the flours used as well as some pertinent information about them. Note: It is important to realize that while many of my recipes are wheat-free/ have wheat-free options, not all of them are gluten-free as even wheat-free flours may contain gluten or are paired with ones that do for baking.

Amaranth flour

A flavorful flour with a taste reminiscent of Amaretto (well known liqueur) that adds flavor to baked goods and acts as a thickening agent. It can be used as a substitute for cornstarch in recipes like pie filling. Not often used alone. Can be found at health food stores.

* **DIY: Amaranth Flour**

Grind amaranth in a grinder until a smooth flour is formed. (Note: this won't form perfectly smooth flour, but it is appropriate for the recipes in which I call for amaranth flour.)

Cornmeal

A tasty flour that is often used to prevent sticking or to add flavor in baked goods. Rarely used alone. Gluten-free. Can be found at most grocery stores.

Oat flour

A soft flour good for cookies, pancakes, and pie crusts that is rather delicate. Not usually gluten-free, although gluten-free varieties can be bought. Make your own using rolled oats and the directions below.

* **DIY: Oat flour**

Grind rolled oats in a grinder until smooth, soft flour is formed.

Spelt flour

A tasty flour that often replaces wheat in baking. As a general rule, for every 1 cup wheat flour, use 1 cup + 2 tbsp spelt flour and an extra 1/8 tsp of baking soda and an extra 1/8 tsp baking powder. Not gluten-free, although some people with Celiac disease can tolerate its gluten. Can be found at super markets and health food stores.

Whole wheat pastry flour/White whole wheat flour

A 100% whole grain flour made using a softer variety of wheat than regular whole wheat flour that yields superior results (compared to regular whole wheat flour) in baked goods such as muffins, brownies, and cakes. Not gluten-free. Can be found in some grocery stores, supermarkets, and health food stores.

Filo Pastry Dough

Sometimes known as Phyllo pastry dough, filo is sold in thin sheets in the freezer section of grocery stores. Check the ingredients for hydrogenated oils, which should be avoided. Whole grain filo pastry dough is available, although harder to find. It is possible to make your own, but requires quite a bit of experience with pastry, so I do not describe the method here.

Looking for kale? See Leafy Greens.

Looking for lentils? See Legumes.

Leafy Greens

Throughout this book, you will find recipes that call for leafy greens such as spinach, collard greens, and kale. These leafy greens are full of important nutrients, but can be hard to find in some regions. There is no need for concern- simply trade one green for another in any given recipe. Remember to always wash greens thoroughly before using them in a recipe and feel free to add a handful to your favorite recipes that are compatible with greens, even if there are not any greens included in the original recipe.

Legumes

I use a variety of legumes in my recipes including chickpeas (also known as garbanzo beans), black (turtle) beans, lentils (red and green), pinto beans, yellow split peas, and black-eyed peas. These legumes are very healthy (lots of fiber, iron, and protein in legumes) and can be used to make a variety of delicious dishes. I highly recommend buying dried legumes and cooking them according to the Bean Cooking Chart on p. 10 not only to economize money, but to ensure well-cooked beans as the quality of some canned beans can vary.

Mango

This luscious, juicy, tropical fruit has a yellow interior and green/red/yellow exterior. It is used to add fruity flavor to savory dishes as well as sweet ones. Mango is widely available in North American supermarkets and grocery stores. A mango is ripe and ready for cutting when its peel is a reddish color and when it is soft and fragrant, but not "squishy". To cut a mango, take a clean mango and slice it twice down the middle, carefully avoiding the oblong pit. You should now have two mango halves and a slim, separate piece containing the pit. You can discard the pit. Now, using a knife, cut a criss-cross pattern into the meat of the remaining mango halves, carefully avoiding cutting through the peel. Turn the mango halves inside out so you get a mango "hedgehog". Carefully cut the mango pieces off the peel. You now have chopped mango ready for use in recipes or ready for an impromptu snack. This method may seem a bit confusing but after a little practice, cutting a mango is no big deal.

Marinara Sauce

In many recipes (pasta especially), I call for prepared marinara sauce (tomato sauce). I personally usually use store-bought marinara sauce, which I find convenient for everyday meals. That being said, not all store-bought sauces are equal. Look for sauces that contain only tomatoes, olive oil, garlic, and salt. These sauces will work well with any recipe you are preparing and are healthier than their corn syrup laden counterparts. If you wish to make your own marinara sauce however, you may do that too.

Millet

Millet is a small, ancient grain that boasts being a source of a variety of vitamins and minerals. It can be bought at some supermarkets and health food stores. It is gluten-free and can be used in place of rice in recipes, if desired. For information on how to cook millet, see the grain cooking chart on p. 11.

Nut/Seed Butter

In this cookbook, I use nut and seed butters (cashew, almond, peanut, tahini) to add nutrients and flavor to recipes. In dessert recipes, nut butters act as an "egg replacer" and help to leaven baked goods, all the while adding rich undertones of flavor. If nut allergies are a concern, equal amounts of seed butter (such as sunflower seed butter or soy nut butter) can be used instead, but be sure to adjust the amount of sweetener and liquid in a recipe if substituting nut butter with seed butter (seed butters aren't a sweet as nut butters).

* **DIY: Nut/Seed Butter**

  To make your own nut/seed butter, grind 2 cups of your desired unsalted nut/seed into a paste using a grinder. Add canola oil (if necessary) to the paste until the mixture is smooth and creamy. Add salt and apple juice concentrate (if making a seed butter) to taste. Makes 1 cup.

* **DIY: Tahini (sesame seed butter)**

  To make your own tahini, spread 4 cups sesame seeds on a baking tray and toast them at 350° F for about 10 minutes, shaking the tray occasionally. Next, transfer the seeds to a grinder and blend them with 1/3 cup canola oil until smooth. Makes 3 cups.

Nutritional Yeast

Nutritional yeast is a flavorful, nutritious powder that is enriched in vitamins and minerals and is high in protein. Make sure to use the Red Star brand nutritional yeast, as it is the only one fortified with B12. It should not be mistaken for brewer's yeast or yeast extract. It is sold in flakes or powder at health food stores. I like to fill an empty spice container with nutritional yeast and keep it on the kitchen table so I can sprinkle it on foods like pasta and cooked vegetables.

Pomegranate

Pomegranates are a type of round fruit with a peel similar to an orange, but that is a purple/red color. They contain sweet, juicy, edible seeds that look like gems to the eye. Pomegranates are now widely available in grocery stores and supermarkets. To prepare one, have ready a mixing bowl full of cold water and a knife with cutting board. Place the pomegranate on the cutting board and cut off the "crown" (top part) and the bottom of the pomegranate. Cut the pomegranate into quarters. Submerge each pomegranate quarter in the water and start to work the seeds out of the membrane. As you work out the seeds, place them aside in a small bowl. Make sure none of the inedible membrane is left on the seeds and that all the seeds are plump and red in color. Note: The inedible membrane should float to the top of the mixing bowl so that you can easily discard it.

Looking for rice milk? See Alternative Milk.

Roasted Red Bell Pepper

Roasted peppers add flavor and richness to many dishes, including soups, pastas, and burgers. You can buy roasted peppers packed in oil, but I recommend roasting them yourself (see below) as it takes very little time and is easy and convenient to do.

* **DIY: Roasted Red Bell Pepper**

  To roast a red bell pepper, slice a clean pepper in half and remove the seeds. Place the pepper halves cut-side down on a baking tray or ovenproof plate and broil them in a toaster oven until the tops of the peppers are blackened. Remove from oven and let cool before chopping into pieces.

Rutabaga

A rutabaga (called a turnip in some regions) is a type of round, yellow, winter root vegetable that keeps well and contains a variety of vitamins and minerals. It boasts being one of the few, fresh vegetables available during the winter in North America. To prepare it for cooking, peel off the purplish exterior (often coated with wax) and cut the rutabaga into the form called for.

Sun-dried Tomatoes

Sun-dried tomatoes add rich flavor and taste to a variety of dishes. Buy them packed in oil rather than air packed; they have more flavor when packed in oil. You can reserve the leftover oil from the tomatoes and use it for sautéing vegetables instead of using olive oil. I use this technique to make leafy greens more appealing (See Vegetable Kale Stir fry, p. 51).

Sweet Potato

There is a lot of confusion over what a sweet potato is and if it is identical to a yam or not. In fact, many grocery stores do not correctly label the two vegetables. Sweet potatoes are smaller then yams and have a bright, orange flesh while yams are larger and sweeter and have a more white flesh. For convenience, I have decided to call the orange fleshed tuber (the only one used in my recipes) that we often see in pie and stew a sweet potato as I feel this is the way it is most often labelled. In some recipes, I do call for having baked the sweet potato beforehand, so below is a way to do so. The same method can be used for regular baking potatoes.

* **DIY: Baked Sweet Potato**
  To bake sweet potatoes, poke holes into them using a fork, place them on a baking tray, and bake them at 375º F for about an hour or until fork tender.

Quinoa

Quinoa is a tiny, ancient grain that cooks up in a way similar to rice, but in less time. Quinoa boasts being a good source of protein and being a source of vitamin E, thiamin, riboflavin, vitamin B6, folate, magnesium, phosphorus, potassium, zinc, copper, manganese, and selenium among others. You can buy quinoa at health food stores and bulk food stores, as well as in the health food section of some grocery stores. To learn how to cook quinoa as well as many other grains, see the grain cooking chart on p. 11.

Vegetable Broth

Vegetable broth is used as a flavorful alternative to water in many recipes. You can find vegetable broths easily at most grocery stores, but since these broths are expensive and high in sodium, it is preferable to make your own following the instructions below.

* **DIY: Vegetable Broth**
  To make your own vegetable broth, sauté one onion, 5 garlic cloves, 3 stalks of celery, and 3 chopped carrots as well as any additional desired vegetable in a tbsp of heated olive oil for about five minutes. Then add 8 cups of light colored bean cooking water and/or vegetable cooking water (or water) 2 tsp soy sauce, one bay leaf, and salt and nutritional yeast to taste. Bring to a boil and let boil rapidly for 5 minutes before lowering heat to medium. Let simmer for about 45 minutes. Strain vegetables and use broth in desired recipe. Makes 8 cups.

Worcestershire sauce

Worcestershire sauce is typically used to flavor beef, but it can also be used in dressings, burgers, and more. I recommend buying vegetarian Worcestershire sauce over regular Worcestershire sauce as it tends to be made with healthier ingredients. You can buy it at health food stores or large grocery stores. Some people make their own Worcestershire sauce but I do not describe the method here.

Wheat Germ

Wheat germ is often added to smoothies, burgers, and baked goods in order to boost their amounts of thiamin, phosphorus, zinc, manganese, and selenium. You can buy them at most grocery stores in the cereal products' section. You will need to use toasted wheat germ for the recipes in this book, so I have included directions for toasting wheat germ below.

* **DIY: Toasted Wheat Germ**
   Place the wheat germ on a baking tray in a thin layer and toast it at 350° F, shaking occasionally, until browned. Watch it carefully to prevent burning.

Whole Grain Bread

Some recipes in this book call for whole grain bread in the form of breadcrumbs or croutons (see below) or recommend serving whole grain bread alongside certain dishes. Not all whole grain bread is equal, so carefully choose it, making sure to choose fresh, locally baked, 100% whole grain breads made with a mixture of grains such as spelt, rye, or other flours. These are the healthiest and tastiest whole grain breads you will find and will yield better results than other breads due to the freshness of the ingredients and the tasty, alternative grains.

* **DIY: Breadcrumbs**
   To make breadcrumbs, tear slices of bread into thumb-sized pieces and grind them into crumbs using a grinder.

* **DIY: Croutons**
   Cut five slices of whole grain bread into cubes and toss them with olive oil (1 to 2 tbsp). Layer the cubes on a baking tray and sprinkle with salt and seasonings of choice. Bake the croutons in a 350° F oven for about 15 minutes or until browned.

Looking for whole wheat pastry flour? See Flour.

Wild Rice Mix

A blend of different types of rice, wild rice mix is used as a wholesome addition to stews and bean burgers. You can find wild rice mix alongside the regular rice at some supermarkets or make it following the directions below. Cook wild rice mixes according to package directions or in the same way you would cook regular brown rice.

* **DIY: Wild Rice Mix**
   Mix 1 part brown rice with 1 part wild rice. Keep in an airtight container in a cool, dry place (such as a pantry).

Handy Measurement Conversion Tables

US Standard	Metric	Imperial
1 tsp	5 ml	.15 ounces
1 tbsp = 3 tsp	15 ml	.5 ounces
1/4 cup	60 ml	2 ounces
1/3 cup	75 ml	3 ounces
1/2 cup	125 ml	4 ounces
2/3 cup	150 ml	5 ounces
3/4 cup	200 ml	6 ounces
1 cup	250 ml	8 ounces
2 cups	500 ml	16 ounces

How to read this table:
1 tsp is slightly over 5 ml and is about equal to .15 of an ounce. *Please note that all conversions are approximate.*

Fahrenheit	Metric (Celsius)
225º F	110º C
250º F	120º C
275º F	135º C
300º F	150º C
325º F	165º C
350º F	175º C
375º F	190º C
400º F	205º C
425º F	220º C
450º F	230º C

All of the oven temperatures in this book are in Fahrenheit.

In all recipes using an oven, the first step is always preheating the oven, even if the recipe calls for overnight preparations. This makes it easy to find the oven temperature in a recipe and lets you easily identify recipes that use an oven.

Dips and Dressings

Creamy Basic Hummus (p. 27)

Guacamole (p. 28)

Dip it!

Dips are amazing- not only can they get everyone eating their fruits and veggies but they can be whipped up in record time. In this chapter, you'll find basic recipes for dips and salsa that will come in handy on a daily basis.

Almondy Carob Fruit Dip

This dip has a rich taste and a smooth texture. It's great for dipping a variety of fruit and for frosting cake.

- **1/3 cup almond butter**
- **1/2 cup apple juice concentrate**
- **1/3 cup carob or cocoa powder**

1. In a mixing bowl, blend the almond butter and juice using a handheld blender.

2. Stir in the carob powder and blend until smooth. This dip will keep for up to a week when refrigerated. Serve!

Makes 8 servings or 1 cup dip

* Add more apple juice for a thinner dip.

* If serving with fruit, generously coat fruit slices with citrus juice to prevent them from browning.

* **Make cashew dip.** Use cashew butter instead of almond butter and ground cashews instead of carob.

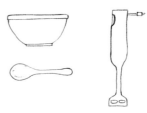

❖ *Flax option: Stir 2 tbsp flax meal into dip before serving. Alternatively, add 2 tsp flax oil to the almond butter before mixing.*

Nutritional Info
(per 1/8 recipe, 24g):

Calories: 91
Fat: 6g (9%)
Sodium: 5mg (0%)
Carbohydrates: 11g (4%)
Fiber: 2g (8%)
Sugars: 7g
Protein: 2g
Omega 3: 42.5mg
Riboflavin: 5% (.1mg)
Niacin: 2% (.4mg)
B6: 2% (.0mg)
Folate: 2% (7.4mcg)
Calcium: 4% (41.6mg)
Iron: 3% (.6mg)
Magnesium: 8% (32.9mg)
Phosphorus: 6% (55.6mg)
Potassium: 5% (166mg)
Zinc: 2% (.3mg)
Copper: 6% (.1mg)
Manganese: 13% (.3mg)

Creamy Basic Hummus

Hummus is a Middle Eastern dip made from chickpeas. This basic recipe makes a creamy, plain hummus that can be used as a vegetable dip or as a spread.

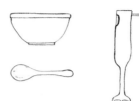

- **2 cups cooked chickpeas, skins removed**
- **1/4 cup water**
- **1/4 cup lemon juice**
- **2 tbsp olive oil**
- **2 tbsp tahini**
- **1/2 tsp balsamic vinegar**
- **3 roasted garlic cloves**
- **Pinch of cumin, chili powder, and ground ginger**
- **Salt to taste**
- **Olive oil and roasted pine nuts for garnishing**

1. In a medium-sized mixing bowl, puree the chickpeas and water until very smooth using a handheld blender.

2. In a small mixing bowl, whisk together the lemon juice, oil, tahini, and vinegar. Add this mixture to the pureed chickpeas along with garlic and seasonings. Puree until very smooth.

3. Transfer hummus to a serving bowl and garnish it with olive oil and pine nuts. Serve!

Makes 8 servings or 2 cups dip

 Removing the chickpea skins is a tedious but worthwhile task that gives you a smooth, creamy hummus.

* Try adding flavorful add-ins (such as sun-dried tomatoes and roasted red bell peppers) when you puree the chickpeas and vegetable broth.

Nutritional Info
(per 1/8 recipe, 63g):

Calories: 123
Fat: 6g (10%)
Sodium: 8mg (0%)
Carbohydrates: 13g (4%)
Fiber: 4g (14%)
Sugars: 2g, Protein: 4g
Omega 3: 58.8mg
VC: 7% (4.1mg)
VE: 3% (.6mg),
VK: 5% (3.7mcg)
Thiamin: 7% (.1mg)
Riboflavin: 3% (.07mg)
Niacin: 2% (.4mg)
B6: 4% (.1mg)
B5: 2% (.2mg)
Calcium: 4% (.2mg)
Iron: 9% (1mg)
Magnesium: 6% (24mg)
Phosphorus: 10% (98.5mg)
Potassium: 4% (148mg)
Zinc: 5% (.8mg)
Copper: 11% (.2mg)
Manganese: 25% (.5mg)
Selenium: 2% (1.7mcg)

{ **To roast garlic**, take a garlic bulb and cut the "pointy" end off. Brush the cut-side with oil, place the bulb cut-side down on a baking tray, and bake it for 1 hour at 350° F. Let cool. }

Guacamole

This is a basic recipe for guacamole, the ever-popular avocado dip. In addition to being used as a dip, it can serve as a sandwich spread and as a condiment for a variety of food.

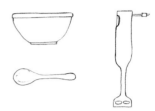

- **1 avocado, peeled and diced**

- **Juice of 1/2 lime**

- **1/2 tsp olive oil**

- **Pinch of salt**

- **Cilantro, fresh or dried, to taste (optional)**

- **Chili powder to taste**

1. In a small mixing bowl, blend the avocado and lime into a chunky puree (or into desired consistency) using a handheld blender. Stir in the olive oil and salt. Season to taste. Serve!

Makes 4 servings

* The olive oil helps keep the avocado from browning.
If you are serving the guacamole immediately, you can leave it out.

* If desired, add a bit of finely diced tomato to your guacamole.

Nutritional Info
(per 1/4 recipe, 56g):

Calories: 87
Fat: 8g (12%)
Sodium: 4mg
Carbohydrates: 5g (2%)
Fiber: 3g (14%)
Protein: 1g
Omega 3: 60mg
VA: 2% (76.1 IU)
VC: 11% (6.7mg)
VE: 6% (1.1mg)
VK: 14% (10.9mcg)
Thiamin: 2% (.07mg)
Riboflavin: 4% (.1mg)
Niacin: 4% (.9mg)
B6: 7% (.1mg)
Folate: 10% (41.3mcg)
B5: 7% (.7mg)
Iron: 2% (.3mg)
Magnesium: 4% (15mg)
Phosphorus: 3% (26.9mg)
Potassium: 7% (250mg)
Zinc: 2% (.3mg)
Copper: 5% (.1mg)
Manganese: 4% (.1mg)

{ **Make your own tortilla chips** by cutting corn tortillas (one tortilla per person) into eighths and placing them on a baking tray. Brush both sides of each tortilla with olive oil and sprinkle them with salt. Bake them at 350° F for 10 minutes or until crispy. }

Salsa

This basic recipe for salsa can be used in any recipe where salsa is called for or as a topping for a variety of foods such as bean burgers.

- **2 large tomatoes, finely chopped**

- **1/2 onion, finely chopped (optional)**

- **1/2 green bell pepper, chopped**

- **2 jalapenos, finely chopped (optional)**

- **1/2 tbsp lime juice**

- **2 garlic cloves, minced**

- **Pinch cumin**

- **Salt, black pepper, and cilantro (fresh or dried) to taste**

1. In a medium-sized mixing bowl, mix the tomatoes, onion, peppers, cilantro, lime juice, garlic, and seasonings.

2. Cover the mixing bowl with plastic wrap and let the salsa chill in the refrigerator for a few hours. Serve!

Makes 4 large servings

 Raw onion has a strong taste that not everyone likes.
Feel free to reduce the onion in this recipe or cut it out all together.
The same can be done with the jalapenos, which are quite hot.

❖ *Flax option:* Stir a few teaspoons of flax oil into salsa before serving.

Nutritional info
(per 1/4 recipe, 84g):

Calories: 20
Fat: 0g
Sodium: 4mg (0%)
Carbohydrates: 5g (2%)
Fiber: 1g
Sugars: 2g
Protein: 1g
VA: 11% (556IU)
VC: 30% (4.1mg)
VE: 2% (.6mg)
VK: 9% (3.7mcg)
Thiamin: 3% (.1mg)
Niacin: 2% (.4mg)
B6: 5% (.1mg)
Folate: 3% (12.6mcg)
Iron: 2% (.3mg)
Magnesium: 3% (10.1mg)
Phosphorus: 2% (22.6mg)
Potassium: 5% (191mg)
Copper: 3% (.1mg)
Manganese: 6% (.1mg)

Thousand Island Dressing (p. 34)

Dress it Up!

Dress things up- with dressing! Dressings have many uses, which not only include their obvious use - dressing salads - but also jazzing up steamed vegetables, coating pasta and beans, and bread dip. They are very convenient as the ingredients that dressing recipes call for are pantry staples and preparing the dressing consists of one simple step - blending the ingredients.

The following recipes are a collection of both basic and more original dressings suitable for everyday use.

Basic Cocktail Dressing

I've dubbed this dressing a "cocktail" dressing because of its combination of typical salad dressing ingredients that form a 'deluxe' version of basic dressing when combined. I like to use this dressing as a bread dip.

- **1 tbsp olive oil**

- **1 tbsp canola oil**

- **1 tbsp lemon juice**

- **1 tsp balsamic vinegar**

- **1 tsp red wine vinegar**

- **3/4 tsp apple juice concentrate**

- **1 tsp prepared mustard**

- **1/2 tsp Italian seasoning**

- **Black pepper and salt to taste**

1. In a small mixing bowl, whisk the oils, lemon juice, vinegars, apple juice, mustard, and seasonings together using a whisk. Serve!

Makes 4 servings

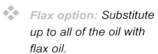

❖ *Flax option: Substitute up to all of the oil with flax oil.*

Nutritional Info
(per 1/4 recipe, 15g):

Calories: 66
Fat: 7g
Sodium: 15mg (1%)
Carbohydrates: 1g (0%)
Sugars: 1g
Omega 3: 353mg
VC: 3% (1.7mg)
VE: 6% (1.1mg)
VK: 7% (5.6mcg)

Cashew Dressing

This tasty salad dressing can be used as a dip for veggies.

- **2 tbsp cashew butter**

- **Juice of 1/2 lemon**

- **1 tsp capers**

- **1/2 tsp Montreal steak spice**

- **1 1/2 tbsp olive oil**

- **1/2 tbsp apple cider vinegar**

- **1/2 tsp apple juice concentrate**

- **2 garlic cloves, roasted**

1. In a small mixing bowl, blend the cashew butter, lemon juice, capers, Montreal steak spice, oil, vinegar, apple juice, and garlic until smooth using a handheld blender. Serve!

Makes 4 serving

* This salad dressing is on the thick side. To make a thinner dressing, add 1 tbsp of cold water at step 1.

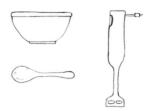

❖ *Flax option: Substitute up to all of the oil with flax oil.*

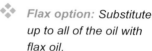

Nutritional Info
(per 1/4 recipe, 23g):

Calories: 96
Fat: 9g (14%)
Sodium: 21mg (1%)
Carbohydrates: 3g (1%)
Fiber: 0g
Sugars: 0g
Protein: 2g
Omega 3: 53.7mg
VC: 5% (.7mg)
VE: 4% (.7mg)
VK: 4% (3.2mcg)
Thiamin: 2% (.0mg)
B6: 2% (.0mg)
Folate: 2% (6.4mcg)
Iron: 3% (.5mg)
Magnesium: 5% (21.7mg)
Phosphorous: 4% (39.4mg)
Potassium: 2% (58.6mg)
Zinc: 3% (.4mg)
Copper: 9% (.2mg)
Manganese: 5% (.1mg)
Selenium: 2% (1.1mcg)

Thousand Island Dressing

Thousand Island Dressing is a blend of mayo and ketchup that's popular in the U.S. It's used not only as a salad dressing, but as a sandwich condiment too. In my version of Thousand Island Dressing, lentils make a healthy substitute for mayo without compromising flavor.

- **1/3 cup cooked red lentils**
- **2 tbsp ketchup**
- **1 tbsp olive oil**
- **2 tsp cashew butter**
- **2 tsp lemon juice**
- **1 tsp sweet relish**
- **Cayenne pepper to taste**

1. In a small mixing bowl, blend the lentils, ketchup, oil, cashew butter, and lemon juice until smooth using a handheld blender.

2. Stir in the sweet relish and cayenne pepper. Serve!

Makes 4 servings

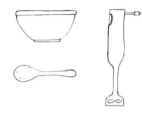

 Flax option: Flax oil can be used instead of olive oil.

Nutritional Info
(per 1/4 recipe, 30g):

Calories: 70
Fat: 5g (7%)
Sodium: 94mg (4%)
Carbohydrates: 6g (2%)
Fiber: 1g
Sugars: 2g
Protein: 2g
Omega 3: 36.4mg
VA: 2% (86.6mg)
VC: 3% (1.9mg)
VE: 3% (.6mg)
VK: 4% (3.5mcg)
Thiamin: 2% (.0mg)
Riboflavin: 2% (.0mg)
Niacin: 2% (.3mg)
B6: 2% (.0mg)
Folate: 7% (29.4mcg)
Iron: 4% (.7mg)
Magnesium: 3% (13.1mg)
Phosphorus: 4% (40.4mg)
Potassium: 3% (98.3mg)
Zinc: 2% (.3mg)
Copper: 5% (.1mg)
Manganese: 5% (.1mg)

Veggie Drizzling Oil

This quick, simple little oil has many uses. In addition to topping steamed veggies, this dressing can be used for dipping bread, coating pasta, and topping cooked vegetables like corn on the cob and mashed potatoes.

- **2 tbsp olive oil**

- **1/2 tsp Italian seasoning**

- **1/2 tsp nutritional yeast**

1. In a mixing bowl, combine the olive oil, Italian seasoning, and nutritional yeast using a whisk. Serve!

Makes 4 servings
(1 serving = enough to pour over 1/2 to 1 cup steamed veggies)

 Flax option: Flax oil can be used instead of olive oil.

Nutritional Info
(per 1/4 recipe, 8g):

Calories: 64
Fat: 7g (10%)
Sodium: 0mg (0%)
Carbohydrates: 0g (0%)
Fiber: 0g
Sugars: 0g
Protein: 1g
Omega 3: 52.3mg
VE: 5% (.1mg)
VK: 6% (5.1mcg)
Thiamin: 40% (.6mg)
Riboflavin: 35% (.6mg)
Niacin: 18% (3.5mg)
B6: 30% (.6mg)
Folate: 4% (15.2mcg)
B12: 8% (.5mcg)
Selenium: 2% (1.4mcg)

Side Dishes

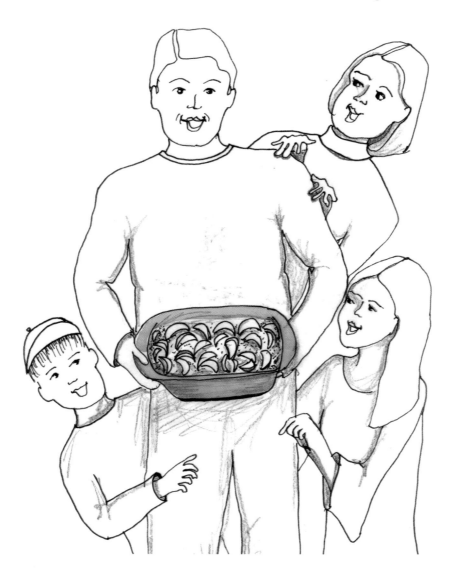

Oven Roasted Potatoes (p. 47)

Sweet Potato Pie (p.50)

Handy Helpers

Side dishes are awfully handy - they help round off a meal and they take little time to prepare. The accompaniments listed here are no exception. They are sure to please.

Baked Sweet Potato Fries

This healthy alternative to French fries is made using sweet potatoes and is baked in the oven.

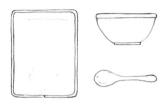

- **2 medium sweet potatoes, peeled and cut into French fry shapes (about 5 cups)**

- **1 1/2 tbsp olive oil**

- **1 1/2 tbsp orange juice concentrate**

- **1 tsp Worcestershire sauce (preferably vegetarian)**

- **1/4 tsp chili powder (optional)**

- **1/2 tsp onion powder**

- **1/2 tsp garlic powder**

- **Salt and black pepper to taste**

1. Preheat the oven to 450° F. Pour 1/2 tbsp of the olive oil onto a baking tray and preheat it in the oven until the oil is hot.

2. In a mixing bowl, mix the sweet potatoes, remaining oil, orange juice, Worcestershire sauce, and seasonings. Cover with plastic wrap and let marinate in the refrigerator for about 30 minutes. (optional step)

3. Remove baking the tray from the oven and spread a layer of fries onto it. Return it to the oven and bake for about 30 minutes or until the potatoes are thoroughly cooked and look roasted. Serve!

Makes 4 servings

* Vegetarian Worcestershire sauce can be found be found at your local health food store or supermarket. You can make your own, although I find it is more practical to use bottled Worcestershire sauce. You can omit it all together, but the fries will lose some of their yummy tanginess.

Nutritional Info
(per 1/4 recipe, 76g):

Calories: 112
Fat: 5g (8%)
Sodium: 38mg (2%)
Carbohydrates: 16g (5%)
Fiber: 2g
Sugars: 5g
Protein: 1g,
Omega 3: 41mg
VA: 186% (9287IU)
VC: 15% (9mg)
VE: 5% (1mg)
VK: 6% (4.4mg)
Thiamin: 5% (.1mg)
Riboflavin: 3% (.0mg)
Niacin: 2% (.4mg)
B6: 8% (.2mg)
Folate: 4% (15.9mcg)
B5: 5% (.5mg)
Calcium: 2% (23mg)
Iron: 3% (.5mg)
Magnesium: 5% (18.8mg)
Phosphorus: 4% (36.4mg)
Potassium: 8% (264mg)
Copper: 5% (.1mg)
Manganese: 9% (.2mg)

Coconut for Potato Scallops

This yummy twist on potato scallops (which is my mother's recipe) is very tasty. I especially like it served with spicy main dishes or soups.

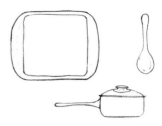

- **4 medium-sized potatoes, peeled and sliced**

- **2 tbsp whole wheat pastry flour**

- **Ground cardamom and ground thyme to taste**

- **1/2 onion, sliced**

- **2/3 cup coconut milk**

- **1/2 cup water**

1. Preheat the oven to 350° F.

2. Layer half the potatoes in an oiled 8 x 8 pan. Layer on all of the onions and then top with the remaining potatoes.

3. Sprinkle the flour, thyme, and cardamom onto the potatoes, and pour the coconut milk and water over potatoes. Cover the dish with aluminium foil.

4. In the preheated oven, cook the potato scallops for 30 minutes or until fork tender. Serve!

Makes 4 servings

 Try using sweet potatoes instead of regular baking potatoes and adding paprika for an interesting twist.

 Flax option: If you wish, sprinkle flax meal on top of the potatoes before serving.

Nutritional Info
(per 1/4 recipe, 209g):

Calories: 240
Fat: 7g (11%)
Sodium: 13mg (1%)
Carbohydrates: 41g (14%)
Fiber: 3g
Sugars: 3g
Protein: 5g
Omega 3: 16.1
VC: 35% (20.9mg)
Thiamin: 12% (.2mg)
Riboflavin: 2% (.0mg)
Niacin: 12% (2.4mg)
B6: 25% (.5mg)
Folate: 5% (113mcg)
B5: 9% (.5mg)
Calcium: 2% (42.6mg)
Iron: 11% (3mg)
Magnesium: 14% (121mg)
Phosphorus: 11% (281mg)
Potassium: 20% (401mg)
Zinc: 4% (2mg)
Copper: 21% (.4mg)
Manganese: 26% (1.5mg)

Curried Quinoa Pilaf

This quick and easy pilaf makes a wonderful accompaniment to many different main dishes.

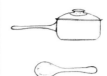

- **1/2 tbsp olive oil**
- **1 onion, chopped**
- **2 garlic cloves, minced**
- **3/4 cup chopped celery**
- **3 cups vegetable broth**
- **1 tsp lemon zest**
- **1 1/2 tsp curry powder**
- **1 tsp dried parsley**
- **1/2 tsp ground ginger**
- **Pinch paprika and cinnamon**
- **2 tbsp raisins (optional)**
- **2 cups rinsed, dry quinoa**
- **Toasted pecans, for garnishing (about 1/4 cup)**

1. Heat the oil in a medium-sized pot. Sauté the onion, garlic, and celery for about 5 to 7 minutes or until tender.

2. Mix in the vegetable broth, zest, seasonings, raisins, and quinoa. Bring to a boil.

3. When boiling, cover the pot and reduce the heat to low. Let the mixture simmer for about 15 to 20 minutes or until the quinoa is cooked (Quinoa is cooked when its "tail" is released.). Stir in the toasted pecans. Serve!

Makes about 6 servings

 Most quinoa needs to be soaked and rinsed before cooking to remove its natural, bitter coating, however some companies pre-rinse their quinoa, so check the package to make sure.

Nutritional Info
(per 1/6 recipe, 198g):

Calories: 269
Fat: 8g (12%)
Sodium: 626mg (26%)
Carbohydrates: 41g (14%)
Fiber: 6g
Sugars: 2g
Protein: 9g
Omega 3: 230mg
VA: 8% (407IU)
VC: 3% (1.6mg)
VE: 9% (1.8mg)
VK: 8% (6.2mcg)
Thiamin: 16% (.2mg)
Riboflavin: 12% (.2mg)
Niacin: 5% (1mg)
B6: 16% (.3mg)
Folate: 28% (113mcg)
B5: 5% (.5mg)
Calcium: 4% (42.6mg)
Iron: 17% (3mg)
Magnesium: 30% (121mg)
Phosphorus: 28% (281mg)
Potassium: 11% (401mg)
Zinc: 14% (2mg)
Copper: 20% (.4mg)
Manganese: 73% (1.5mg)
Selenium: 8% (5.4mcg)

Fruit 'n Nut Couscous Pilaf

This recipe is easy to prepare and makes for a side dish that's sure to wow and please. Serve it alongside a spicy main dish for a balanced harmony of flavors.

- **1 1/2 cups vegetable broth**
- **4 green onions, chopped**
- **3/4 tsp ground ginger**
- **1 tbsp olive oil, plus extra for drizzling**
- **1 cup dry whole wheat couscous**

    ❀ *Gluten-free option: Use millet/quinoa instead of couscous and cook accordingly.*

- **1 1/2 cup chopped mango**
- **1/3 cup slivered almonds**
- **2 tbsp dried cranberries**
- **2 tbsp orange juice concentrate**
- **Cayenne pepper and black pepper to taste**
- **Olive oil for drizzling (optional)**

1. In a medium-sized pot, mix the broth, onion, ginger, and oil. Bring to a boil.

2. Stir the couscous into boiling water and set aside, covered with a lid, until all the liquid is absorbed. Fluff couscous with a fork.

3. Mix the mango, almonds, cranberries, and mango juice into cooked couscous. Season the couscous to taste with cayenne and black pepper and drizzle it with oil, if desired. Serve!

Makes 6 servings

✳ Look for whole wheat couscous in large supermarkets or health food stores.

✳ If mango isn't available, Clementine pieces can be substituted.

❖ *Flax option: Drizzle with flax oil instead of olive oil.*

Nutritional Info
(per 1/6 recipe, 149g):

Calories: 236
Fat: 6g (9%)
Sodium: 307mg (13%)
Carbohydrates: 43g (14%)
Fiber: 7g
Sugars: 10g
Protein: 7g
Omega 3: 32.3mg
VA: 15% (756IU)
VC: 23% (13.6mg)
VE: 11% (2.2mg)
VK: 20% (16.4mcg)
Thiamin: 3% (.0mg)
Riboflavin: 5% (.1mg)
Niacin: 2% (.5mg)
B6: 3% (.1mg)
Folate: 2% (8.8mcg)
Calcium: 4% (39.8mg)
Iron: 9% (1.6mg)
Magnesium: 5% (19.5mg)
Phosphorus: 3% (33.1mg)
Potassium: 3% (117mg)
Copper: 5% (.1mg)
Manganese: 8% (.2mg)

Lemony Asparagus Rice

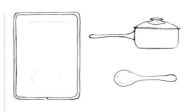

This recipe is easily the best side dish ever. After being broiled, the rice is crunchy and flavorful and the asparagus is tasty and tender. Mmmm…

- **4 cups cooked brown rice**

- **2 cups chopped asparagus, steamed**

- **2 tbsp soy sauce**

- **1 tbsp olive oil**

- **Juice of one lemon**

- **Roasted pecans or almonds for garnishing (optional)**

1. Put oven on high broil setting.

2. Toss together the rice, asparagus, soy sauce, oil, and juice in a medium-sized mixing bowl and transfer the mixture to an oiled baking tray.

3. Broil for 5 to 10 minutes in the preheated oven or until the top of the rice is crunchy. Remove from oven and sprinkle roasted nuts (if desired) on top of the dish. Serve!

Makes 4 to 6 servings

 Try using cooked quinoa or millet instead of rice.

 If you wish, snow peas could be used instead of asparagus.

Nutritional Info
(per 1/5 of recipe, 229g):

Calories: 217
Fat: 4g (6%)
Sodium: 411mg (17%)
Carbohydrates: 39g (13%)
Fiber: 4g
Sugars: 2g
Protein: 6g
Omega 3: 48.1mg
VA: 8% (407IU)
VC: 12% (7.3mg)
VE: 5% (1.1mg)
VK: 31% (24.9mcg)
Thiamin: 16% (.2mg)
Riboflavin: 7% (.1mg)
Niacin: 16% (3.2mg)
B6: 15% (.3mg)
Folate: 9% (36.6mcg)
B5: 6% (.6mg)
Calcium: 3% (30.6mg)
Iron: 11% (2mg)
Magnesium: 20% (78mg)
Phosphorus: 17% (167mg)
Potassium: 6% (202mg)
Zinc: 9% (1.3mg)
Copper: 13% (.3mg)
Manganese: 77% (1.5mg)
Selenium: 24% (16.6mcg)

Lentil Rice Pilaf

This quick pilaf adds a punch of healthy proteins and whole grains to your meal.

- **1 cup dry brown rice**

- **1/2 cup dry green lentils**

- **3/4 tsp Italian seasoning**

- **Seasoning salt, black pepper, and cayenne pepper to taste**

- **Pinch cumin, garlic powder, and dried parsley**

- **2 1/2 cups vegetable broth**

- **Olive oil and lemon juice for dressing**

- **Toasted nuts (pecans, cashews, almonds; use your favorite) for garnishing**

1. In a medium-sized pot, mix the rice, lentils, seasonings, and broth. Bring the mixture to a boil, then cover it, and reduce the heat to low.

2. Let simmer for about twenty to thirty minutes or until all the broth is absorbed. Remove from heat, fluff, and drizzle with olive oil and lemon juice. Garnish with toasted nuts. Serve!

Makes about 4 servings

 You could try using millet or quinoa in place of rice, if desired.

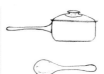

 Flax option: Use flax oil in place of olive oil in the dressing.

Nutritional Info
(per 1/4 recipe, 211g):

Calories: 269
Fat: 2g (2%)
Sodium: 768mg (32%)
Carbohydrates: 53g (18%)
Fiber: 10g
Sugars: 2g
Protein: 60g
VA: 8% (416IU)
VC: 2% (1.1mg)
VK: 2% (1.2mcg)
Thiamin: 27% (.4mg)
Riboflavin: 4% (.1mg)
Niacin: 13% (2.7mg)
B6: 19% (.4mg)
Folate: 31% (124mcg)
B5: 12% (1.2mg)
Calcium: 3% (29.1mg)
Iron: 15% (2.7mg)
Magnesium: 24% (97.2mg)
Phosphorus: 23% (234mg)
Potassium: 10% (356mg)
Zinc: 14% (2.1mg)
Copper: 13% (.3mg)
Manganese: 105% (2.1mg)
Selenium: 3% (2mcg)

Lovely Lentil Salad

This flavorful, unique lentil salad makes good use of all of lentils' fine points. Try doubling this recipe and making it ahead so you can use it as a side dish throughout the week.

- **2 tbsp olive oil**

- **2 tbsp balsamic vinegar**

- **1 tsp dried basil**

- **1/2 tsp ground savory**

- **1/8 tsp dried dill**

- **Black pepper and paprika to taste**

- **2 cups cooked green lentils**

- **2/3 cup chopped red bell pepper**

- **2/3 cup chopped celery**

1. In a medium-sized mixing bowl, whisk the oil, vinegar, and seasonings together with a fork.

2. Stir the lentils, pepper, and celery into dressing mixture. Cover the bowl with plastic wrap and chill in the refrigerator until cold. Serve!

Makes 4 servings

* Black-eyed peas, chickpeas, kidney beans, and black beans could all be used in place of lentils in this recipe.

 Flax option: Use flax oil in place of olive oil.

Nutritional Info
(per 1/4 recipe, 161g):

Calories: 194
Fat: 7g (11%)
Sodium: 20mg (1%)
Carbohydrates: 23g (8%)
Fiber: 9g
Omega 3: 95mg
VA: 20% (978IU)
VC: 63% (37.8mg)
VE: 5% (1.6mg)
VK: 13% (12.7mcg)
Thiamin: 12% (.2mg)
Riboflavin: 6% (.1mg)
Niacin: 7% (1.4mg)
B6: 14% (.3mg)
Folate: 50% (199mcg)
B5: 8% (.8mg)
Calcium: 3% (34.5mg)
Iron: 20% (3.6mg)
Magnesium: 11% (42.8mg)
Phosphorus: 19% (192mg)
Potassium: 14% (485mg)
Zinc: 9% (1.4mg)
Copper: 13% (.3mg)
Manganese: 28% (.6mg)
Selenium: 4% (2.9mcg)

Oven Roasted Potatoes

This simple, traditional dish is always a favorite.

- **4 large potatoes, peeled and chopped into cubes (equivalent of 4 cups)**

- **2 garlic cloves, minced**

- **2 tbsp olive oil**

- **1/2 tsp salt**

- **Seasonings and herbs to taste (Montreal steak spice, rosemary…)**

1. Preheat the oven to 375° F.

2. In a large mixing bowl, mix the potatoes, garlic, oil, and salt. Make sure potatoes are well-coated with olive oil. Sprinkle them with desired seasonings.

3. Cover the mixing bowl with plastic wrap and marinate the potatoes for 30 minutes up to an entire day (This step is optional).

4. Spread the potatoes in a single layer on an oiled baking tray and bake them for about 30 minutes in the preheated oven or until they are thoroughly cooked. Serve!

 You can use this recipe to make oven roasted vegetables. Use about 5 cups of chopped veggies such as brussels sprouts, rutabaga, turnip, red bell pepper, carrots, squash, sweet potatoes, eggplant, zucchini, and tomatoes instead of the four potatoes and follow the recipe above. You may add 2 to 4 tbsp of lemon juice or balsamic vinegar to the recipe if desired.

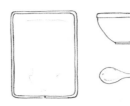

 You can use yellow, red or Russet potatoes in this recipe. Sweet potatoes can also be used.

Nutritional Info
(per 1/4 recipe, 165g):

Calories: 208
Fat: 7g
Sodium: 299mg (12%)
Carbohydrates: 34g (11%)
Fiber: 2g
Sugars: 3g
Protein: 3g
Omega 3: 67.4mg
VC: 34% (1.6mg)
VE: 5% (.6mg)
VK: 6% (4.6mcg)
Thiamin: 11% (.2mg)
Riboflavin: 2% (.0mg)
Niacin: 11% (2.2mg)
B6: 25% (.5mg)
Folate: 4% (14.1mcg)
B5: 9% (.9mg)
Iron: 3% (.6mg)
Magnesium: 10% (39.6mg)
Phosphorus: 8% (81.4mg)
Potassium: 18% (619mg)
Zinc: 3% (.5mg)
Copper: 17% (.3mg)
Manganese: 14% (.3mg)

Rutabaga Slaw

This rutabaga-apple slaw is tossed with a light vinegar and canola oil dressing to keep things healthy and tasty.

- **1 1/2 cup shredded rutabaga**
- **1/2 cup shredded red-skinned apple of any kind (roughly one apple)**
- **1 tbsp apple cider vinegar**
- **1 tbsp canola oil**
- **1 tsp prepared mustard**
- **Cumin to taste (optional)**
- **Fresh herbs to garnish (optional)**

1. In a mixing bowl, toss the shredded rutabaga and apple. Set aside.

2. In a smaller bowl, whisk together the vinegar, mustard, and oil. Stir the dressing into the rutabaga mixture. Season with cumin and garnish with fresh herbs. Chill for at least 30 minutes before serving. Serve!

Makes 4 servings

 You can shred the rutabaga and apple by hand, but it is much more efficient to use a food processor with a shredding setting.

 To make a carrot salad using this recipe, replace the rutabaga with carrots and the vinegar with lemon juice and add 1/3 cup raisins and 3 tbsp pecans. Omit cumin and thyme.

❖ *Flax option: Replace canola oil with flax oil.*

Nutritional Info
(per 1/4 recipe, 75g):

Calories: 59
Fat: 4g (5%)
Sodium: 11mg (0%)
Carbohydrates: 6g (2%)
Fiber: 2g
Sugars: 5g
Protein: 1g
Omega 3: 120mg
VC: 23% (13.8mg)
VE: 4% (.9mg)
Thiamin: 3% (.0mg)
Niacin: 2% (.4mg)
B6: 3% (.1mg)
Folate: 3% (11.5mcg)
Calcium: 3% (25.9mg)
Iron: 2% (.3mg)
Magnesium: 3% (13mg)
Phosphorus: 3% (32.5mg)
Potassium: 6% (196mg)
Manganese: 5% (.1mg)

Starring Celery Salad

Poor old celery never seems to get to be the star! Give this unappreciated veggie a chance to shine with this 100% celery salad. This relish-style salad is great alongside bean burgers and whole grain bread.

- **1 tbsp olive oil**

- **1 tbsp balsamic vinegar**

- **1/2 tsp prepared mustard**

- **1 tsp Worcestershire sauce (preferably vegetarian)**

- **1/4 tsp celery seed**

- **1 tsp dried basil**

- **Pinch garlic powder**

- **Cayenne pepper, salt, and black pepper to taste**

- **2 cups chopped celery**

1. In a medium-sized mixing bowl, whisk together the oil, vinegar, mustard, Worcestershire sauce, and seasonings.

2. Stir in the celery. Cover the bowl with plastic wrap and chill until cool. Serve!

Makes 4 servings

 Vegetarian Worcestershire sauce can be found be found at your local health food store or supermarket. You can make your own, although I find it is more practical to use bottled Worcestershire sauce.

❖ *Flax option:* Use flax oil instead of olive oil.

Nutritional Info
(per 1/4 recipe, 60g):

Calories: 44
Fat: 4g (5%)
Sodium: 69mg (3%)
Fiber: 1g
Sugars: 2g
Protein: 0g
Omega 3: 33.7mg
VA: 5% (227IU)
VC: 3% (1.6mg)
VE: 3% (.6mg)
VK: 28% (16.8mcg)
Riboflavin: 2% (.0mg)
B6: 2% (.0mg)
Folate: 5% (18.2mcg)
Calcium: 3% (21.7mg)
Magnesium: 2% (6.3mg)
Potassium: 4% (137mg)
Manganese: 3% (.1mg)

Sweet Potato Pie

Making this tasty pie has become a holiday tradition for our family. Its creamy texture and comforting taste make it a favorite. It's great served with cranberry sauce.

Crust:

- **1 2/3 cups oats**
- **Pinch of salt**
- **1/2 cup coconut milk**
- **5 tbsp water**

Filling:

- **3 medium-sized sweet potatoes, baked and peeled**
- **2 tbsp almond butter**
- **3 tbsp orange juice concentrate**
- **1 1/2 tsp cinnamon**
- **Pinch of nutmeg**

 To bake a sweet potato, follow the directions on page 19.

Nutritional Info
(per 1/8 recipe, 97g):

Calories: 166, Fat: 6g (10%)
Sodium: 31mg (1%)
Carbohydrates: 25g (8%)
Fiber: 4g
Sugars: 4g
Protein: 4g
Omega 3: 34.2mg
VA: 139% (6937IU)
VC: 14% (8.6mg)
VK: 2% (1.4mcg)
Thiamin: 9% (.1mg)
Riboflavin: 5% (.1mg)
Niacin: 4% (.7mg)
B6: 7% (.1mg)
Folate: 6% (23.3mcg)
B5: 6% (.6mg)
Calcium: 4% (43mg)
Iron: 9% (1.7mg)
Magnesium: 14% (55.3mg)
Phosphorus: 13% (127mg)
Potassium: 9% (322mg)
Zinc: 6% (1mg)
Copper: 11% (.2mg)
Manganese: 50% (1mg)
Selenium: 7% (5mcg)

1. Preheat the oven to 375° F.

2. In a grinder, grind the oats into flour. Transfer the flour to a small mixing bowl and stir in the salt. Make a well in the center of the flour and pour in the coconut milk and water. Combine, and then press the dough evenly and firmly into an oiled pie tin. Brush the pie crust with extra coconut milk, cover it with plastic wrap, and refrigerate it (to prevent drying).

3. In a medium-sized bowl, use a handheld blender to puree the sweet potatoes. Stir in the almond butter, orange juice, cinnamon, and nutmeg and blend until smooth.

4. Pour the filling into the pie crust and brush the edges of the pie crust with canola oil. Bake in the preheated oven for about 45 minutes or until the crust is thoroughly cooked. Let cool. Serve!

Makes 8 servings

If you wish, you can use a more traditional pie crust that the crust crust above, but make sure to choose a crust free of hydrogenated oils.

{ **To make homemade cranberry sauce**, combine 2 parts fresh cranberries to 1 part orange juice concentrate (chopped Clementine pieces can be added if desired) and 1 part date puree in a medium-size pot. Bring the mixture to a boil and let it simmer until all the berries "pop". Simmer to the desired consistency. This can be stored up to a week in the fridge. }

Vegetable Kale Stir-fry

This simple stir-fry is my favorite way to eat super vegetable kale. The sun-dried tomato oil used in this dish is the key to its good taste.

- **1 tbsp sun-dried tomato oil**

- **1 onion, chopped**

- **1 1/2 cup carrots, chopped**

- **2 cups cauliflower florettes**

- **6 cups kale stems, chopped and steamed in a steam broiler**

- **Toasted almonds as garnish**

1. In a skillet, Heat the oil and sauté the onion, carrots, and cauliflower for 5 to 7 minutes.

2. Add the kale and cook the stir-fry until all the vegetables are tender. Remove from heat and garnish with toasted almonds. Serve!

Makes 4 servings

✳ The Sun-dried tomato oil called for here is referring to the oil sun-dried tomatoes are packed in. This oil usually has a more flavorful taste than regular oil and really adds a lot to this dish.

✳ Kale can be replaced by other leafy greens such as spinach or collard greens. I recommend steaming these greens (with the exception of spinach) before hand in a steam broiler as I find this keeps the stir-fry from getting "soggy".

Nutritional Info
(per 1/4 serving, 190g):

Calories: 91
Fat: 4g (6%)
Sodium: 64mg (3%)
Carbohydrates: 13g (4%)
Fiber: 4g
Sugars: 5g
Protein: 3g
Omega 3: 113 mg
VA: 339% (16880IU)
VC: 90% (53.9mg)
VE: 7% (548mcg)
VK: 685% (548mcg)
Thiamin: 7% (.1mg)
Riboflavin: 6% (.1mg)
Niacin: 5% (1.1mg)
B6: 15% (.3mg)
Folate: 12% (49.6mcg)
B5: 5% (.5mg)
Calcium: 8% (78.8mg)
Iron: 6% (1mg)
Magnesium: 7% (27.5mg)
Phosphorus: 7% (65.2mg)
Potassium: 14% (492mg)
Zinc: 3% (.5mg)
Copper: 8% (.2mg)
Manganese: 23% (.5mg)
Selenium: 2% (1.1mcg)

Main Dishes

Red Lentil Beanballs (p. 61)

Green Power Lentil Burgers (p. 59)

Legummm...

The tasty legume dishes in this chapter are sure to make you go mmmm… Here you'll find burgers, loaves, beanballs, and more that are sure to please your taste buds and your body - legumes are a good source of protein and of many vitamins and minerals.

Cooking with Legumes: Q & A

What does it mean to "partially puree" beans or blend them into a "chunky paste"?

When I call for "partially pureeing" or putting legumes in a "chunky paste" in a burger, beanball, or loaf recipe, I mean for the beans to be pureed into a moist paste that isn't completely smooth and that has about 1/4 cup of the beans still whole and not pureed.

What type of breadcrumbs should I use for burger/beanball/loaf recipes?

I always use fresh breadcrumbs in my recipes as I find they have a better taste than store-bought ones (plus, they're not filled with additives and preservatives). Fresh breadcrumbs cannot be substituted with store-bought breadcrumbs as their moisture content and texture is not the same. To make your own breadcrumbs, tear slices of whole grain bread into thumb sized pieces and grind into crumbs using a grinder.

Can I cook homemade bean burgers on the grill?

Grilling bean burgers on the grill can be tricky as they are a good deal more delicate than meat burgers, but it is possible. I recommend adding 1 to 2 tbsp wheat gluten flour (available at most grocery stores and supermarkets) to the burger mixture so that the burgers "hold" together more and freezing them before attempting to cook them on the grill.

What can I serve homemade beanballs and burgers with?

Homemade beanballs can be served with ketchup/salsa or Spicy Cashew Sauce *(p. 62)* on top of a cooked grain such as rice or on top of pasta covered with pasta sauce. Burgers can be served with store-bought whole grain burger buns or with Basic Pizza Crust (burger bun variation) on p. 80. They can be topped with ketchup and mustard, Salsa and Guacamole *(p. 28 and 29)*, or with Spicy Cashew Sauce *(p. 62)*. Tomatoes, lettuce and red onions can be served with burgers as well.

How can I freeze homemade burgers and beanballs?

You can freeze burgers and bean balls by placing them on a baking tray and then covering them with plastic wrap. Freeze them until solid, then remove them from the baking tray, and store them in an airtight plastic container in the freezer for later use.

Back To Basics Burgers

These burgers are quite tasty and their quick prep time and no fuss ingredients make them a great "fall-back-meal" for times when time is short and a trip to the grocery store is looming.

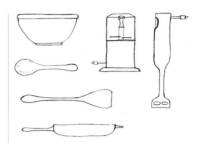

- **2 cups cooked black beans**

- **2/3 cup walnuts**

- **2 1/2 tbsp tomato paste**

- **1/2 tsp onion powder**

- **1/2 tsp garlic powder**

- **2 tsp nutritional yeast**

- **Cayenne pepper, cumin to taste**

- **1 cup cooked brown rice**

- **2 tsp olive oil**

1. In a medium-sized mixing bowl, puree the black beans into a partial puree using a handheld blender.

2. In a grinder, grind the walnuts into a paste. Add the walnuts to the black bean mixture along with the tomato paste and seasonings. Stir in the rice.

3. Divide the mixture into four equal parts and form it into burgers using your hands.

4. Heat the oil in a skillet. Cook the burgers about 4 minutes on each side. Remember that while these hold together well, if you're used to flipping meat burgers you'll have to be more delicate. Serve!

Makes 4 burgers.

✳ If you wish, 2 green onions (chopped) 1/4 cup grated carrots, or 1/4 cup cooked corn can be stirred in at step two.

Nutritional Info
(per 1/4 recipe, 166g):

Calories: 299
Fat: 12g (19%)
Sodium: 16mg (1%)
Carbohydrates: 37g (12%)
Fiber: 10g
Sugars: 2g
Protein: 13g
Omega 3: 6965mg
VA: 4% (192IU)
VC: 5% (3mg)
VE: 3% (.7mg)
VK: 3% (2.1mcg)
Thiamin: 67% (1mg)
Riboflavin: 46% (.8mg)
Niacin: 28% (5.7mg)
B6: 47% (.9mg)
Folate: 41% (166mcg)
B12: 9% (.6mcg)
B5: 5% (.5mg)
Calcium: 5% (51.6mg)
Iron: 16% (2.9mg)
Magnesium: 29% (116mg)
Phosphorus: 25% (246mg)
Potassium: 16% (554mg)
Zinc: 14% (2.1mg)
Copper: 28% (.6mg)
Manganese: 73% (1.5mg)
Selenium: 13% (9mcg)

Ginger Black-eyed Pea Bake

This bean bake gets its unique flavor from its original combination of ingredients: black-eyed peas, roasted red pepper, raisins, and ginger. The top of the bake is covered with a tasty ginger crumb topping. The fact that this bake bubbles in the oven all day while you stay at ease knowing supper is ready is a great plus.

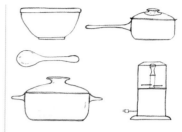

- **2 cups dry black-eyed peas, soaked overnight in water**

- **5 cups water or vegetable broth**

- **3 tbsp tomato paste**

- **1 onion, chopped**

- **2 tsp Italian seasoning**

- **1/2 tsp ground ginger**

- **1/2 tsp Montreal steak spice**

- **Paprika, black pepper, and salt to taste**

- **1 red bell pepper, roasted (p. 18) and chopped**

- **3 tbsp raisins**

- **1 slice whole grain bread**

- **1/4 cup roasted cashews**

- **1 tsp ground ginger**

1. Preheat the oven to 225° F. In a large pot, mix the black-eyed peas, water, tomato paste, onion, and seasonings (excluding 1 tsp ground ginger). Bring the mixture to a boil. Reduce the heat and simmer for about 20 to 30 minutes.

2. Transfer the black-eyed peas to a large casserole dish. Stir in the red pepper and raisins. From here, you can either refrigerate the casserole overnight and continue with the recipe the next morning or go immediately to the next step.

3. Bake the beans, well-covered with the baking dish's lid, for about 7 hours. Remove from oven.

4. In a grinder, grind the bread, cashews, and 1 tsp ground ginger into a uniform mixture. Top the beans with the breadcrumb mixture and return them to the oven, uncovered, for about 15 minutes. Serve!

Makes 8 servings

 If desired, chickpeas can be used instead of black-eyed peas in this recipe.

Nutritional Info
(per 1/8 recipe, 262g):

Calories: 204
Fat: 4g (6%)
Sodium: 797mg (33%)
Carbohydrates: 37g (12%)
Fiber: 6g
Sugars: 17g
Protein: 7g
Omega 3: 29.2mg
VA: 19% (965IU)
VC: 38% (22.6mg)
VE: 3% (.7mg)
VK: 6% (5.1mcg)
Thiamin: 6% (.1mg)
Riboflavin: 4% (.1mg)
Niacin: 4% (.8mg)
B6: 7% (.1mg)
Folate: 4% (16.7mcg)
B5: 2% (.2mg)
Calcium: 2% (23.7mg)
Iron: 15% (2.6mg)
Magnesium: 9% (37.2mg)
Zinc: 4% (.6mg)
Copper: 13% (.3mg)
Manganese: 20% (.4mg)
Selenium: 6% (4.2mcg)

Green Power Lentil Burgers

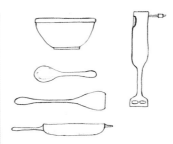

These lentil burgers are spotted with color because of the carrots, onions, and peas they contain. With their simple yet tasty combination of different foods, these burgers are sure to find a place at your dinner table.

- **2 cups cooked green lentils**

- **1/3 cup raw sunflower seeds**

- **1/2 cup toasted wheat germ**

    ◆ *Wheat-free option:* *Use 3/4 cup wheat-free, whole grain breadcrumbs instead of wheat germ*

- **1/2 onion, finely chopped or 2-3 green onions, finely minced**

- **1/2 cup shredded carrot**

- **1/2 cup frozen green peas, cooked**

- **1/2 tsp garlic powder**

- **1 tsp nutritional yeast**

- **1/2 tsp dried thyme**

- **2 tsp olive oil**

1. In a medium-sized mixing bowl, puree the green lentils into a partial puree using a handheld blender. Stir in the onion, carrots, peas, and seasonings. Use a handheld blender to blend the vegetables into the mixture, keeping it chunky, yet uniform.

2. In a grinder, grind the sunflower seeds into a paste. Stir the paste and wheat germ into the lentil mixture.

3. Divide the mixture into 4 equal parts and form burgers.

4. Heat the oil in a skillet. Place the burgers on the skillet and cook for about 5 minutes on each side or until golden brown. Serve!

Makes 4 servings

 This recipe can also be made into beanballs that can be served falafel-style inside whole grain pitas. After step two, follow directions for Red Lentil Beanballs (on p. 61) starting at step 5.

Nutritional Info
(per 1/4 recipe, 157g):

Calories: 212
Fat: 5g (8%)
Sodium: 29mg (1%)
Carbohydrates: 30g (10%)
Fiber: 11g
Sugars: 4g, Protein: 13g
Omega 3: 115 mg
VA: 60% (2982IU)
VC: 9% (5.2mg)
VE: 8% (1.7mg)
VK: 15% (12mcg)
Thiamin: 70% (1.1mg)
Riboflavin: 46% (.8mg)
Niacin: 30% (6mg)
B6: 51% (1mg)
Folate: 60% (240mcg)
B12: 9% (.5mcg)
B5: 10% (.3mg)
Calcium: 4% (68mg)
Iron: 25% (4mg)
Magnesium: 18% (84.5mg)
Phosphorus: 30% (231mg)
Potassium: 16% (395mg)
Zinc: 18% (2mg)
Copper: 20% (.4mg)
Manganese: 81% (1.5mg)
Selenium: 17% (3.9mcg)

Indian Spiced Quinoa Rolls

These elegant rolls are great for fancier dinners. Their great flavor is worth the celebration. Serve with an elegant side salad, perhaps made with romaine lettuce.

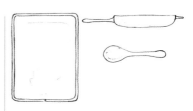

- **1 onion, chopped**
- **1/2 red bell pepper, chopped**
- **1 cup shredded carrot**
- **2 cups cooked chickpeas**
- **2 cups cooked quinoa (p. 19)**
- **1/2 tbsp olive oil**
- **1 clove garlic, minced**
- **1/2 tsp Garam Masala**
- **Cumin and basil to taste**
- **1/2 tsp soy sauce**
- **1/4 cup pine nuts, ground into a meal**
- **12 sheets of filo pastry**

1. Preheat the oven to 375° F.

2. In a skillet, Heat the oil and sauté the garlic and onion for about 3 minutes. Add the carrots, bell pepper, and chickpeas. Sauté for 5 more minutes before adding the quinoa and seasonings. Let mixture cool to prevent the filo pastry from melting.

3. Layer 2 sheets of filo pastry on a baking tray and cut the sheets in half to form 2 rectangular pieces of pastry. Repeat this step for the rest of the filo pastry.

4. Form the rolls. Divide the quinoa mixture into sixths. Place one sixth of the mixture horizontally at the short side of a pastry sheet, about 1 to 2 inches away from the edge. Roll it up carefully and tuck in the edges. Set aside. Repeat until you have finished the quinoa mixture.

5. Place all the rolls on an oiled baking tray and bake them in the preheated oven for 15 minutes or until the filo pastry is browned. Serve!

Makes 6 servings (1 roll= 1 serving).

* Garam Masala is a blend of Indian spices that can be found at some grocery stores and supermarkets.

* If you wish, this dish can be made without filo pastry and simply served as a warm grain dish.

Nutritional Info
(per 1/6 recipe, 186g):

Calories: 307
Fat: 9g
Sodium: 190mg (8%)
Carbohydrates: 47g (16%)
Fiber: 8g
Sugars: 6g
Protein: 12g
Omega 3: 41.7mg
VA: 68% (3393IU)
VC: 26% (15.3mg)
VE: 8% (1.5mg)
VK: 11% (8.8mg)
Thiamin: 12% (.2mg)
Riboflavin: 8% (.1mg)
Niacin: 5% (1.1mg)
B6: 11% (.2mg)
Folate: 33% (132mcg)
B5: 3% (.3mg)
Calcium: 7% (68mg)
Iron: 22% (4mg)
Magnesium: 21% (84.5mg)
Phosphorus: 23% (2.31mg)
Potassium: 11% (395mg)
Zinc: 13% (2mg)
Copper: 20% (.4mg)
Manganese: 75% (1.5mg)
Selenium: 6% (3.9mcg)

Red Lentil Beanballs

Great over pasta, rice, as a finger food, or in a sandwich, these tasty bites will please anyone.

- **2/3 cup dry red lentils**
- **2 cups water or tomato juice**
- **1/3 cup walnuts**
- **3/4 cup fresh breadcrumbs (p. 56)**
- **1 tsp Italian seasoning**
- **1/2 tsp dried basil**
- **1/2 tsp garlic powder**
- **1 tsp nutritional yeast**
- **Pinch cumin**
- **1 tsp olive oil**

1. Preheat the oven to 375° F.

2. In a small pot, simmer the lentils with water or juice until soft (15 to 20 minutes). They should look almost pureed. Delicately drain liquid from the lentils using a sieve.

3. Grind the walnuts into a paste in a grinder. Place them in a mixing bowl and add the breadcrumbs and seasonings. Stir in the lentils.

4. Now, form small balls out of the mixture, using about 1 tbsp for each ball. Place the balls on an oiled baking tray. Pour olive oil into a small dish and use a basting brush to lightly coat the beanballs with oil.

5. Bake the beanballs in the preheated oven for about 15 minutes or until golden brown. Serve!

Makes 6 servings (24 beanballs)

* If desired, sauté 1/2 onion, 1/4 cup shredded carrots, and 1/4 cup celery and add at step 3.

❖ *Flax option: Stir in 2 tbsp flax meal at step 3.*

Nutritional Info
(per 1/6 recipe, 102g):

Calories: 203
Fat: 6g (10%)
Sodium: 99mg (4%)
Carbohydrates: 29g (10%)
Fiber: 8g Sugars: 2g
Protein: 10g
Omega 3: 652mg
VC: 2% (1.2mg)
VE: 2% (.4mg)
VK: 8% (6.2mcg)
Thiamin: 43% (.6mg)
Riboflavin: 32% (.5mg)
Niacin: 22% (4.3mg)
B6: 32% (.6mg)
Folate: 39% (154mcg)
B12: 6% (.3mcg)
B5: 6% (.6mg)
Calcium: 3% (30.3mg)
Iron: 18% (3.3mg)
Magnesium: 14% (57.1mg)
Phosphorus: 20% (200mg)
Potassium: 11% ((377mg)
Zinc: 11% (1.6mg)
Copper: 17% (.3mg)
Manganese: 53% (1.1mg)
Selenium: 20% (14mcg)

Savory Beanballs & Spicy Cashew Sauce

These savory, little beanballs take no time to make and are great served over rice topped with Spicy Cashew Sauce, below.

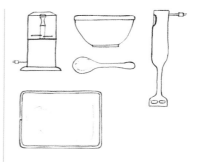

For the beanballs:

- **2 cup cooked black-eyed peas**
- **1/2 cup sliced mushrooms**
- **1/2 cup shredded carrots**
- **1 cup fresh breadcrumbs (p. 56)**
- **1/2 cup walnuts**
- **1 tsp dried oregano**
- **1 tsp dried thyme**
- **Salt and black and cayenne pepper to taste**
- **1 tsp olive oil**

For the sauce:

- **3/4 cup roasted cashews**
- **3/4 tsp of McCormick's Montreal Steak Spice**
- **3/4 tsp garlic powder**
- **1 tbsp olive oil**
- **5 tbsp vegetable broth**
- **Black pepper, Salt** (unless salted cashews were used) **and cayenne pepper to taste**

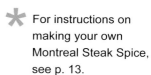

For instructions on making your own Montreal Steak Spice, see p. 13.

❖ *Flax option: Stir in 2 tbsp of flax meal at step 3.*

1. Preheat the oven to 375° F.

2. In a grinder, grind walnuts into a paste. Set aside.

3. In mixing bowl, use a handheld blender to partially puree the black-eyed peas and mushrooms. Stir in the carrots, breadcrumbs, walnuts, and seasonings.

4. Now, form small balls out of the mixture, using about 1 tbsp bean mixture for each ball. Place the balls on an oiled baking tray. Pour olive oil into a small dish and use a basting brush to lightly coat the beanballs oil.

5. Bake the beanballs in the preheated oven for about 15 minutes or until golden brown. While the beanballs are baking, prepare the cashew sauce: Grind the cashews into a paste in a grinder. Add the oil, seasonings, and vegetable broth and blend until smooth. Drizzle the sauce over the beanballs. Serve!

Makes 6 servings (24 beanballs)

✳ You may need to add a good deal more liquid to the cashew sauce if the cashews you are using aren't freshly roasted. Add additional liquid gradually, adding 1 tbsp vegetable broth first and then 1 tbsp oil until desired consistency is reached.

Nutritional Info
(per 1/4 recipe, 142g):

Calories: 325
Fat: 19g (29%)
Sodium: 104mg (4%)
Carbohydrates: 31g (10%)
Fiber: 7g, Sugars: 5g
Protein: 12g
Omega 3: 976 mg
VA: 31% (1569IU)
VC: 3% (1.9mg)
VE: 3% (.9mg)
VK: 17% (13.6mcg)
Thiamin: 12% (.2mg)
Riboflavin: 6% (.1mg)
Niacin: 7% (1.4mg)
B6: 9% (.2mg)
Folate: 7% (28.4mcg)
B5: 4% (.4mg)
Calcium: 3% (33.4mg)
Iron: 22% (3.9mg)
Magnesium: 21% (85.2mg)
Phosphorus: 19% (187mg)
Potassium: 8% (285mg)
Zinc: 11% (1.7mg)
Copper: 32% (.6mg)
Manganese: 48% (1mg)
Selenium: 16% (11.5mcg)

Savory Lentil Loaf

This yummy loaf has plenty of tasty ingredients including sun-dried tomatoes and mushrooms. This loaf makes a nice, filling meal.

- **1 tsp olive oil**
- **2 garlic cloves, minced (p. 19)**
- **1/2 onion, finely chopped**
- **1 1/2 cup sliced mushrooms**
- **3 cups cooked green lentils**
- **12 sun-dried tomatoes (in oil)**
- **1 cup fresh breadcrumbs (p. 56)**
- **1/2 cup walnuts**
- **2 tbsp ketchup**

- **1 tsp prepared mustard**
- **1/2 tbsp peanut butter**
- **1/2 tsp garlic powder**
- **1/2 tsp onion powder**
- **1/2 tsp dried rosemary**
- **3/4 tsp dried thyme**
- **2 tbsp nutritional yeast**
- **Seasoning salt and black pepper to taste**

1. Preheat the oven to 350° F.

2. Heat the oil in a skillet and sauté the onion, garlic, and mushrooms for about 7 minutes or until tender.

3. In a medium-sized mixing bowl, puree the lentils and sun-dried tomatoes into a partial puree. Mix in the mushroom mixture, breadcrumbs, ketchup, mustard, peanut butter, and seasonings.

4. Grind the walnuts into a paste in a grinder. Stir into the lentil mixture.

5. Transfer the lentil mixture to an oiled loaf pan. Firmly and evenly press the mixture into an oiled loaf pan. Bake in the preheated oven for an hour or a toothpick comes out slightly sticky. Serve!

Makes 6 servings

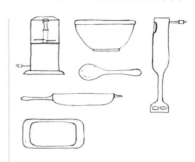

❖ *Flax option: Stir in 2 tbsp of flax meal at step 4.*

Nutritional Info
(per 1/6 recipe, 175g):

Calories: 281
Fat: 10g (16%)
Sodium: 86mg (4%)
Carbohydrates: 36g (12%)
Fiber: 12g
Sugars: 3g
Protein: 16g
Omega 3: 989mg
VA: 2% (96.9IU)
VC: 15% (8.9mg)
VE: 3% (.5mg)
VK: 8% (6.6mcg)
Thiamin: 207% (3.1mg)
Riboflavin: 181% (3.1mg)
Niacin: 98% (19.6mg)
B6: 157% (3.1mg)
Folate: 70% (279mcg)
B12: 39% (2.3mcg)
B5: 15% (1.5mg)
Calcium: 5% (50.1mg)
Iron: 27% (4.8mg)
Magnesium: 20% (81.6mg)
Phosphorus: 34% (339mg)
Potassium: 22% (783mg)
Zinc: 20% (3mg)
Copper: 30% (.6mg)
Manganese: 62% (1.2mg)
Selenium: 29% (20.3mcg)

Southern Black-Eyed Pea Loaf

This colorful, yummy loaf is a tribute to southern flavors.

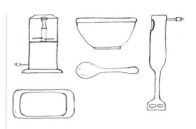

- **2 cups cooked black-eyed peas**
- **1/2 cup chopped celery**
- **1/2 red bell pepper, roasted (p. 18) and chopped**
- **1/2 cup cooked wild rice mix**
- **1/2 cup cashews, ground into a meal**
- **3/4 tsp paprika**
- **1 tsp garlic powder**
- **1/2 tsp onion powder**
- **1 tsp dried thyme**
- **1 tsp dried oregano**
- **Salt and pepper to taste**

1. Preheat the oven to 350° F.

2. In a mixing bowl, mix the black-eyed peas, celery, and pepper and blend them into a chunky puree using a handheld blender.

3. In a grinder, grind the cashews into a paste. Stir them into the bean mixture along with the wild rice and seasonings. Press the mixture firmly and evenly into an oiled loaf pan.

4. Bake the loaf for an hour in the preheated oven or until a toothpick comes out slightly sticky. Serve!

Makes 6 servings

* This recipe can be made into burgers. Simply follow directions up to step three, form into burgers, and cook on a skillet according to the directions for Back To Basics Burgers on p. 57.

Nutritional Info
(per 1/6 recipe, 123g):

Calories: 182
Fat: 7g
Sodium: 19mg (1%)
Carbohydrates: 24g (8%)
Fiber: 5g
Sugars: 3g
Protein: 8g
VA: 13% (648IU)
VC: 26% (15.4mg)
VE: 3% (.7mg)
VK: 22% (17.3mcg)
Thiamin: 9% (.1mg)
Riboflavin: 5% (.1mg)
Niacin: 5% (1mg)
B6: 12% (.2mg)
Folate: 8% (31.2mcg)
B5: 3% (.3mg)
Calcium: 3% (33.4mg)
Iron: 23% (4.2mg)
Magnesium: 21% (82.8mg)
Phosphorus: 18% (176mg)
Potassium: 8% (295mg)
Zinc: 13% (1.9mg)
Copper: 27% (.5mg)
Manganese: 27% (.5mg)
Selenium: 7% (.5mcg)

Speckled Red Pepper Burgers

These cheerful burgers are made with yellow split peas, a legume usually limited to soup.

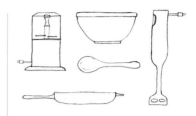

- **2 cups cooked yellow split peas**

- **1/2 cup walnuts**

- **1 cup fresh breadcrumbs (p. 56)**

- **1 red bell pepper, roasted (p. 18) and chopped**

- **1/2 tsp garlic powder**

- **1/4 tsp onion powder**

- **1/2 tsp Montreal steak spice**

- **1/2 tsp dried sage**

- **Seasoning salt and black and cayenne pepper to taste**

1. In a grinder, grind the walnuts into a paste. Set aside.

2. Place the yellow split peas into a medium-sized bowl and using a handheld blender, blend into a chunky puree. Stir in the walnuts, breadcrumbs, pepper, and seasonings.

3. Divide the mixture into 4 parts and form burgers.

4. Heat the oil in a skillet. Cook the burgers for about 5 minutes on each side or until golden brown. Serve!

Makes 4 servings

* These burgers could be made using cooked black beans instead of yellow split peas.

❖ *Flax option: Stir in 2 tbsp flax meal at step 2.*

Nutritional Info
(per 1/4 recipe, 91g):

Calories: 142
Fat: 5g
Sodium: 29mg (1%)
Carbohydrates: 20g (7%)
Fiber: 7g
Sugars: 3g
Protein: 7g
Omega 3: 577mg
VA: 8% (397IU)
VC: 27% (16.3mg)
VE: 2% (.3mg)
VK: 7% (5.5mcg)
Thiamin: 12% (.2mg)
Riboflavin: 4% (.1mg)
Niacin: 5% (1.1mg)
B6: 6% (.1mg)
Folate: 15% (59.3mcg)
B5: 5% (.5mg)
Calcium: 2% (19.8mg)
Iron: 7% (1.3mg)
Magnesium: 10% (41mg)
Phosphorus: 10% (104mg)
Potassium: 9% (317mg)
Zinc: 7% (1mg)
Copper: 12% (.2mg)
Manganese: 31% (.6mg)
Selenium: 5% (3.7mcg)

shown with Starring Celery Salad (p. 49)

Classic Vegetarian Pasta Sauce (p. 71)

Pasta-tively Delicious

Pasta is a staple in many households and that's no wonder considering that it is easy to prepare and appeals to everyone, even picky eaters. Many times however, white pasta is used and the sauces that coat it are unhealthful. The recipes in this chapter will show you that whole grain pastas and healthy sauces are not only good for you, but also very tasty.

Preparing Pasta

How to cook pasta

The following basic instructions will show you how to prepare dried pasta. This method is intended for cooking about 12 to 16 oz of pasta or enough to feed 4 to 6 people.

- Generously fill a large pot with water (The more water you use, the less the pasta will stick.).

- Bring the water to a boil, covered, then remove the lid and stir in pasta and salt (if desired).

- Set a kitchen timer for 8 minutes, as this is usually the minimum amount of time it will take for pasta to cook. If you are using a gluten-free or wheat mix pasta, you may want to stir the pasta during this time to prevent sticking. When the timer beeps, check the pasta. The noodles should be al dente or to the bite. If they are not, continue cooking them, watching them carefully. When they are ready, continue to the next step.

- After reserving a cup of the pasta cooking water, drain the pasta in a colander over the kitchen sink. Do not rinse the pasta. Return it to the original cooking pot, making sure to not place it over a cooling stove. Serve the pasta immediately.

* If you cannot serve the pasta immediately, cover the pasta pot with a lid and stir in a bit of the reserved pasta cooking water every few minutes or so to keep it from drying out.

Making your own fresh pasta:

To make your own fresh pasta, combine a few tablespoons of water with 1 cup of flour (whole wheat pastry flour or semolina with a bit of chickpea flour added to it, if desired) using a mixing spoon and a mixing bowl or a pasta machine. Add more water or flour until the dough is not wet or sticky to the touch and forms thumb-sized clumps. Cut the dough into pasta shapes using a pasta machine or by rolling it out using a rolling pin and cutting it by hand. Cook it according to the directions above, but reduce the cooking time to 2 to 3 minutes and stir continuously. You will have enough pasta to feed 3 to 4 people.

* Ravioli is the best pasta shape for beginners– it yields good results and is easy to make. To make it, lay a sheet of rolled out pasta dough over a mini muffin tin and slightly indent the pasta covering the muffin holes using the back of a spoon. Fill the raviolis with a filling of your choice (I like to use hummus) and then layer on another sheet of pasta. Use a rolling pin to fuse the two sheets of pasta. Cut ravioli out in squares and remove from muffin tin. Cook according to directions above.

* **A Note on Marinara Sauce:** As I said in the beginning of this book, I use bottled marinara sauce for convenience. Again, choose bottled sauces that contain only the basics: tomatoes, olive oil, salt, spices, and herbs. The quality of the marinara sauce can make or break a dish, so choosing your sauce wisely is important.

Autumn Vegetable Pasta Sauce

This sauce is absolutely wonderful. Vibrantly colored due to its inclusion of a variety of fresh vegetables, this sauce's delectable taste and creamy texture is sure to win you over. Serve with whole grain pasta.

- **1/2 tbsp olive oil**

- **1 onion, chopped**

- **1 red bell pepper, chopped**

- **1 cup sliced mushrooms**

- **3 garlic cloves, minced**

- **3 cups pureed butternut squash**

- **2 1/2 cups vegetable broth**

- **2 tsp dried basil**

- **2 tsp dried oregano**

- **2 cups chopped spinach**

- **2 cups cooked chickpeas**

- **Olive oil for drizzling (optional)**

1. Heat the oil in a saucepan and sauté the onion, pepper, mushrooms, and garlic for 5 to 7 minutes.

2. Stir in the squash, vegetable broth, and seasonings. Simmer for 10 to 15 minutes and then add the spinach and chickpeas. Warm the sauce until thoroughly heated and then drizzle with oil, if desired. Serve!

Makes 4 servings

 I like to cook large amounts of butternut squash in the oven at once and use it to prepare this recipe and others, such as Sneaky Butternut Lentil Soup on p. 94. For directions on cooking butternut squash, see p. 14.

Flax option: Drizzle with flax oil rather than olive oil.

Nutritional Info
(per 1/4 recipe, 387g):

Calories: 130
Fat: 2g (3%)
Sodium: 612mg (26%)
Carbohydrates: 28g (9%)
Fiber: 3g
Sugars: 7g
Protein: 4g
Omega 3: 119mg
VA: 454% (22719 IU)
VC: 119% (71.6mg)
VE: 17% (3.5mg)
VK: 105% (84.3mcg)
Thiamin: 13% (.2mg)
Riboflavin: 13% (.2mg)
Niacin: 17% (3.3mg)
B6: 21% (.4mg)
Folate: 26% (87.9mcg)
B5: 12% (1.2mg)
Calcium: 11% (114mg)
Iron: 12% (2.1mg)
Magnesium: 19% (76mg)
Phosphorus: 11% (106mg)
Potassium: 24% (828mg)
Zinc: 4% (.7mg)
Copper: 13% (.3mg)
Manganese: 30% (.6mg)
Selenium: 8% (5.3mcg)

Chunky Oven Pasta Sauce

This flavorful pasta sauce bubbles happily in the oven while you spend the pre-dinner hours savoring its aroma. Made with lots of yummy, earthy veggies like rutabaga, this sauce is quite healthy, too. Serve it over small pasta shapes along with Red Lentil Beanballs on p. 61. This sauce is pictured on the front cover.

- **28 oz can crushed tomatoes**
- **4 cups marinara sauce**
- **1/4 cup coconut milk**
- **1 cup vegetable juice**
- **1 cup sliced mushrooms**
- **1 cup chopped celery**
- **1 green bell pepper, chopped**
- **1 onion, chopped**
- **1 rutabaga, peeled and cubed**
- **2 tsp dried basil**
- **2 tsp dried oregano**
- **1 1/2 tsp dried parsley**
- **1/8 to 1/4 tsp cayenne pepper**
- **1/2 tsp celery seed (optional)**
- **Salt and pepper to taste**
- **Olive oil for drizzling**

1. Preheat the oven to 350° F.

2. In a large casserole dish, mix the tomatoes, sauce, vegetable juice, and coconut milk. Stir in the mushrooms, celery, pepper, onion, rutabaga, and seasonings.

3. Cover the casserole dish with a lid and bake the pasta sauce in the preheated oven for 2 to 3 hours or until the vegetables are fork tender. Remove it from the oven and drizzle it with olive oil. Serve!

Makes 8 servings

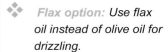

Flax option: Use flax oil instead of olive oil for drizzling.

Nutritional Info
(per 1/8 recipe, 355g):

Calories: 119
Fat: 2g (3%)
Sodium: 107mg (4%)
Carbohydrates: 23g (8%)
Fiber: 5g
Sugars: 12g
Protein: 4g
Omega 3: 43.6mg
VA: 21% (1034IU)
VC: 90% (54.1mg)
VE: 15% (3.1mg)
VK: 21% (16.6mcg)
Thiamin: 14% (.2mg)
Riboflavin: 13% (.2mg)
Niacin: 16% (3.2mg)
B6: 21% (.4mg)
Folate: 10% (41.2mcg)
B5: 5% (.5mg)
Calcium: 9% (94.7mg)
Iron: 16% (2.9mg)
Magnesium: 14% (55.5mg)
Phosphorus: 12% (117mg)
Potassium: 29% (1010mg)
Zinc: 5% (.8mg)
Copper: 20% (.4mg)
Manganese: 23% (.5mg)
Selenium: 5% (3.2mcg)

Classic Vegetarian Pasta Sauce

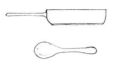

This simple, tasty sauce will grace your table often. Serve it with your favorite type of whole grain pasta and a simple side salad.

- 1/2 tbsp olive oil

- 1 onion chopped

- 2 medium garlic cloves, chopped

- 1/2 cup celery

- 1 cup grated carrot

- 2 cups chopped zucchini

- 1 cup sliced mushrooms

- 3 1/2 cups marinara sauce

- 1 tbsp apple juice concentrate

- 1 tsp dried oregano

- 1 tsp dried basil

- Pinch of ground cardamom

- 2 cups cooked chickpeas

- 1 cup chopped black olives

- Olive oil for drizzling

❖ *Flax option: Use flax oil instead of olive oil for drizzling.*

Nutritional Info
(per 1/6 recipe, 344g):

Calories: 225
Fat: 9g (13%)
Sodium: 1037mg (43%)
Carbohydrates: 33g (11%)
Fiber: 10g
Sugars: 11g
Protein: 9g
Omega 3: 105mg
VA: 116% (5761IU),
VC: 26% (15.3mg)
VE: 17% (3.5mg)
VK: 22% (17.5mcg)
Thiamin: 11% (.2mg)
Riboflavin: 15% (.3mg)
Niacin: 14% (2.8mg)
B6: 17% (.3mg)
Folate: 32% (129mcg)
B5: 6% (.6mg)
Calcium: 14% (135mg)
Iron: 31% (5.5mg)
Magnesium: 19% (76.9mg)
Phosphorus: 19% (193mg)
Potassium: 27% (942mg)
Zinc: 11% (1.6mg)
Copper: 29% (.6mg)
Manganese: 53% (1.1mg)
Selenium: 8% (5.9mcg)

1. Heat the oil in a saucepan. Sauté the onion, celery, and garlic until tender. Then add the carrots and zucchini and sauté for 5 more minutes.

2. Add the mushrooms and sauté for 3 minutes. Stir in the marinara sauce, juice, chickpeas, and olives. Let the sauce simmer for 15 to 20 minutes or until the vegetables are tender. Stir in the herbs and cardamom. Drizzle with olive oil. Serve!

Makes 6 servings

Cruise Ship Pasta

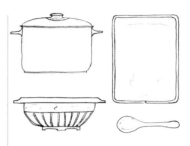

Why is this recipe called Cruise Ship Pasta? Cruise ships are known for their excellent food and this tasty dish can be served in a pineapple "boat".

- **1 or 2 medium pineapples**
- **1 cup chopped pineapple**
- **12 oz dry whole grain pasta shapes, like bow ties**
   Gluten-free option: Use gluten-free whole grain pasta
- **1/4 cup chopped black olives**
- **1/4 cup finely chopped green bell pepper**
- **1/2 cup halved grape tomatoes**
- **1 1/2 cup marinara sauce**
- **1 tsp dried basil**
- **Cayenne pepper, salt, and black pepper to taste.**

1. Fill a large pot 2/3 full with water. Bring to a boil. Add the pasta and salt and boil for about 10 to 12 minutes or until pasta is al dente. Meanwhile, follow steps the below. When the pasta is cooked, drain it and return it to the cooking pot. Set aside.

2. Cut off the top and bottom of the pineapple. Set aside. Slice the middle in half lengthwise. Carefully carve pineapple "meat" out of the middle halves, leaving 3/4 inch border at the borders. Set aside the pineapple "meat".

3. Assemble the boat. Place the top and bottom on opposite sides of a baking tray. One carved-out, middle piece should be placed on the tray so it appears connected to the top. The other piece should be placed so it appears connected to the bottom. The middle pieces should appear connected in the middle. The pineapple shell should look like a long pineapple that has been scooped out in the middle.

4. Mix the pineapple, olives, pepper, tomatoes, marinara sauce, and seasonings into the pasta. Stuff the pineapple by generously filling it with half of the mixture. Replenish it with more pasta later, if necessary. Serve!

Makes 4 servings

* If you wish, omit steps 2 and 3 to make a simple pasta dish that can be served in the traditional way.

Nutritional Info
(per 1/4 recipe, 277g):

Calories: 487
Fat: 4g
Sodium: 133mg (6%)
Carbohydrates: 97g (32%)
Fiber: 13g
Sugars: 14g
Protein: 18g
Omega 3: 22.5mg
VA: 15% (727IU)
VC: 66% (40.6mg)
VE: 10% (1.9mg)
VK: 9% (7.3mcg)
Thiamin: 60% (.9mg)
Riboflavin: 12% (.2mg)
Niacin: 33% (6.6mg)
B6: 11% (.2mg)
Folate: 110% (440mcg)
Calcium: 6% (61.3mg)
Iron: 41% (7.3mg)
Magnesium: 6% (25.4mg)
Zinc: 2% (.3mg)
Copper: 14% (.3mg)
Manganese: 27% (.5mg)

Gingery Pasta Sauce

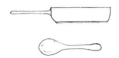

This is a one of a kind sauce with a sweet, gingery taste that makes it a refreshing twist on regular pasta sauce. Serve with whole grain pasta or on top of other whole grains such as millet, quinoa, rice, or whole wheat couscous.

- **1 tsp sesame oil**

- **2 garlic cloves, minced**

- **1 cup chopped carrots**

- **3 cups marinara sauce**

- **2 tbsp freshly grated ginger**

- **1 tbsp apple juice concentrate**

- **1 cup chopped spinach**

- **2 cups cooked chickpeas**

- **Toasted sesame oil for drizzling (optional)**

1. Heat the oil in a saucepan and sauté the garlic and carrots for about 5 minutes.

2. Add the marinara sauce, ginger, and apple juice and simmer rapidly for 15 minutes. Stir in the spinach and chickpeas. When the spinach is cooked, drizzle the sauce with additional oil, if desired. Serve!

Makes 4 servings

✱ If necessary, substitute fresh ginger with 2 tsp ground ginger.

Nutritional Info
(per 1/4 recipe, 319g):

Calories: 286
Fat: 5g (7%)
Sodium: 89mg (4%)
Carbohydrates: 51g (17%)
Fiber: 12g
Sugars: 15g
Protein: 13g
Omega 3: 72.7mg
VA: 162% (8095IU)
VC: 40% (24.2mg)
VE: 16% (3.2mg)
VK: 63% (50.5mcg)
Thiamin: 18% (.3mg)
Riboflavin: 12% (.2mg)
Niacin: 14% (2.7mg)
B6: 25% (.5mg)
Folate: 57% (228mcg)
B5: 5% (.5mg)
Calcium: 11% (106mg)
Iron: 28% (5.1mg)
Magnesium: 24% (95.5mg)
Phosphorus: 26% (257mg)
Potassium: 30% (1043mg)
Zinc: 15% (2.3mg)
Copper: 3% (.7mg)
Manganese: 88% (1.8mg)
Selenium: 9% (6mcg)

Nutrilicious Pasta

This creamy nutritional yeast sauce is reminiscent of cheese sauce. In addition to topping pasta, this sauce can be used on steamed veggies, sandwiches, and much more.

- **16 oz whole grain pasta shapes**

    ❧ *Gluten-free option: Use a gluten-free whole grain pasta*

- **1/2 cup nutritional yeast**

- **1/2 cup flour**

- **1/2 cup water**

- **1/2 cup vegetable broth**

- **2 tbsp cashew butter**

- **1 tsp prepared mustard**

- **1/2 tsp apple juice concentrate**

- **Salt and thyme to taste**

1 Fill a large pot 2/3 full with water. Bring to a boil. Add the pasta and salt and boil for about 10 to 12 minutes or until pasta is al dente. Meanwhile, follow the steps below. When the pasta is cooked, drain it and return it to the cooking pot. Set aside.

3. In a saucepan, whisk the nutritional yeast, flour, water, and vegetable broth together.

4. Heat the mixture over medium-low to medium heat, watching it carefully and stirring often. When the mixture has thickened sufficiently, stir in the cashew butter, mustard, juice, and seasonings.

5. Mix the nutritional yeast sauce into cooked the pasta. (Do not delay serving time; this dish is best served immediately.) Serve!

Makes 4 servings

* If desired, stir in 2 cups of steamed broccoli florettes or cooked green peas at step 5.

Nutritional Info (per 1/4 recipe, 110g):

Calories: 210
Fat: 6g (9%)
Sodium: 224mg (9%)
Carbohydrates: 27g (9%)
Fiber: 8g
Sugars: 0g
Protein: 17g
Omega 3: 23.3mg
VE: 2% (.3mg)
Thiamin: 1137% (17.1mg)
Riboflavin: 996% (16.9mg)
Niacin: 499% (99.8mg)
B6: 846% (16.9mg)
Folate: 115% (462mcg)
B12: 233% (14mcg)
B5: 24% (2.4mg)
Calcium: 9% (92.2mg)
Iron: 20% (3.6mg)
Magnesium: 23% (93.2mg)
Phosphorus: 53% (528mg)
Potassium: 19% (667mg)
Zinc: 46% (6.9mg)
Copper: 30% (.6mg)
Manganese: 97% (1.9mg)
Selenium: 107% (74.9mcg)

Peanutty Pasta

Although this sauce is great on warm pasta, it can serve double duty as a sandwich condiment, salad dressing, vegetable topping, and much more.

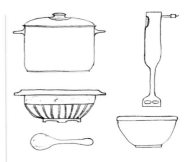

- **16 oz dry whole grain spaghetti, cooked**

  🌿 *Gluten-free option: Use gluten-free whole grain pasta*

- **1/2 cup creamy peanut butter**

- **2 tbsp soy sauce**

- **1 tbsp sesame oil**

- **1/4 cup coconut milk**

- **3 tbsp water**

- **2 garlic cloves**

- **1/4 tsp ground ginger**

- **1/2 lime, juiced**

- **Cayenne pepper to taste**

1. Fill a large pot 2/3 full with water. Bring to a boil. Add the pasta and salt and boil for about 10 to 12 minutes or until pasta is al dente. Meanwhile, make the peanut sauce. When the pasta is cooked, drain it and return it to the cooking pot. Set aside.

2. In a mixing bowl, blend the peanut butter and water using a handheld blender. the Add soy sauce, sesame oil, coconut milk, garlic, ginger, lime juice, and cayenne pepper and puree until smooth.

3. Toss the peanut sauce into the just-cooked pasta. Serve!

Makes 6 servings

✳ You do not need to heat the peanut butter sauce before serving; the heat from the just-cooked noodles will warm the sauce sufficiently.

✳ If you wish, stir in chopped vegetables such as chopped cucumber, shredded carrots, and chopped snow peas at step three to make a more complete meal.

Nutritional Info
(per 1/6 serving, 132g):

Calories: 443
Fat: 17g (26%)
Sodium: 340 mg (14%)
Carbohydrates: 60g (20%)
Fiber: 8g
Sugars: 6g
Protein: 17g
Omega 3: 23.9mg
VA: 2% (89.8IU)
VC: 3% (1.5mg)
VE: 10% (2mg)
Thiamin: 37% (.6mg)
Riboflavin: 7% (.1mg)
Niacin: 34% (6.7mg)
B6: 7% (.1mg)
Folate: 75% (300mcg)
B5: 3% (.3mg)
Calcium: 2% (33.2mg)
Iron: 27% (4.8mg)
Magnesium: 10% (40.7mg)
Phosphorus: 10% (95.9mg)
Potassium: 5% (181mg)
Zinc: 5% (.7mg)
Copper: 7% (.1mg)
Manganese: 22% (.4mg)
Selenium: 2% (1.4mcg)

Red Pepper Extravaganza Pasta

This delicious pasta goes all out with its medley of exquisite ingredients. Try serving it with a vegetable salad of your choice.

- **16 oz whole grain spaghettini or angel hair pasta**

  Gluten-free option: Use gluten-free whole grain pasta

- **1 tbsp olive oil**
- **1 onion, chopped**
- **2 garlic cloves, minced**
- **2 cups sliced mushrooms**
- **1 red bell pepper, roasted (p. 18) and chopped**
- **2 cups cooked chickpeas**
- **1/2 cup homemade croutons (p. 20)**
- **1/4 cup roasted cashews**
- **1/2 cup chopped black olives**
- **2 cups marinara sauce**
- **3 tbsp chopped fresh parsley**

1. Fill a large pot 2/3 full with water. Bring to a boil. Add the pasta and salt and boil for about 10 to 12 minutes or until pasta is al dente. Meanwhile, follow steps two and three. When the pasta is cooked, drain it and return it to the cooking pot. Set aside.

2. Heat the oil in a skillet. Sauté the onion and garlic for 5 to 7 minutes. Add the mushrooms and continue to sauté until they are tender. Mix in the red pepper and chickpeas and sauté for a few more minutes. Set aside.

3. In a grinder, grind the croutons and cashews into a crumbly paste. Set aside.

4. In the pasta cooking pot, toss the pasta and marinara sauce. Add the crouton mixture and combine until evenly distributed. Stir in the sautéed vegetables and parsley. Serve!

Makes 6 servings

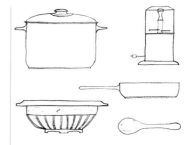

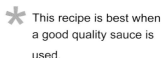

* This recipe is best when a good quality sauce is used.

❖ *Flax option: Add 1 tablespoon of golden flax meal to crouton mixture at step 3.*

Nutritional Info
(per 1/6 recipe, 296g):

Calories: 471
Fat: 7g (11%)
Sodium: 119mg (5%)
Carbohydrates: 85g (28%)
Fiber: 14g, Sugars: 11g
Protein: 19g
Omega 3: 49.3mg
VA: 25% (1267IU)
VC: 67% (40.3mg)
VD: 2% (7.6IU)
VE: 11% (2.1mg)
VK: 49% (38.9mcg)
Thiamin: 49% (.7mg)
Riboflavin: 22% (.4mg)
Niacin: 33% (6.6mg)
B6: 16% (.3mg)
Folate: 103% (411mcg)
B5: 8% (.8mg)
Calcium: 8% (77.8mg)
Iron: 40% (7.2mg)
Magnesium: 17% (66.1mg)
Phosphorus: 20% (197mg)
Zinc: 11% (1.7mg)
Copper: 31% (.3mg)
Manganese: 40% (.5mg)
Selenium: 13% (1.8mcg)

Spinaci Pesto Cream Sauce

Spinaci is the Italian word for spinach. This creamy, pesto-like sauce is a great way to eat your greens. You can serve it on top of whole grain pasta alongside marinara sauce, if desired.

- **1/2 tbsp olive oil**
- **6 cups packed spinach**
- **3/4 cup vegetable broth**
- **3 tbsp cashew butter**
- **1 tsp dried basil**
- **Salt and pepper to taste**

1. In a skillet, heat the oil and sauté spinach until cooked.

2. Transfer the spinach to a mixing bowl and puree until smooth with a handheld blender.

3. Add the basil, vegetable broth, and cashew butter to the spinach and combine using a handheld blender. Reheat if needed. Serve!

Makes 4 servings

Nutritional Info
(per 1/4 serving, 101g):

Calories: 100
Fat: 8g
Sodium: 267mg (11%)
Carbohydrates: 6g (2%)
Fiber: 1g
Sugars: 1g
Protein: 3g
Omega 3: 97.5mg
VA: 88% (4376IU)
VC: 21% (12.8mg)
VE: 6% (1.2mg)
VK: 276% (221mcg)
Thiamin: 5% (.1mg)
Riboflavin: 6% (.1mg)
Niacin: 3% (.5mg)
B6: 6% (.1mg)
Folate: 24% (95.9mcg)
B5: 2% (.2mg)
Calcium: 5% (50.9mg)
Iron: 10% (1.9mg)
Magnesium: 17% (66.9mg)
Phosphorus: 8% (77.3mg)
Potassium: 9% (319mg)
Zinc: 6% (.9mg)
Copper: 16% (.3mg)
Manganese: 25% (.5mg)
Selenium: 3% (1.8mcg)

Lemony Potato Pizza (p. 82)

Pizza Pizazz

Pizza has now become a common household meal in North America. Often laden with unhealthy ingredients and made with a white crust, pizza is usually not a good choice. But don't fear, pizza need not always be a bad choice. In this chapter, you'll find healthy recipes for pizza toppings and pizza crust that keep pizza a good choice that you can enjoy.

Basic Pizza Crust

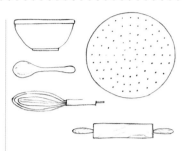

Here is a recipe for a traditional pizza crust that can be garnished with the toppings of your choice.

- **1 1/4 cup warm water**
- **2 1/4 tsp active dry yeast**
- **1 tbsp apple juice concentrate**
- **3 cups whole wheat flour**
- **1/2 tsp salt**

1. Preheat the oven to 400º F.

2. In a mixing bowl, whisk together the water and the yeast until the yeast dissolves. Let rest 5 minutes and meanwhile, mix the salt and flour in a separate bowl.

3. Whisk the juice into the yeast and gradually add the flour. Turn out onto a floured surface and knead for about 15 minutes. Place the dough ball in an oiled medium-sized bowl, cover with a clean dishcloth, and let it rise in a warm place (such as an oven with the light turned on) for an hour and a half or until doubled in size.

4. Punch the dough down. Using a rolling pin, roll the dough out into a 14 inch circle on a floured surface. Poke small holes into the middle of the crust using a toothpick. Dust the crust with cornmeal, place it on a pizza pan, and bake it in the preheated oven for about 10 minutes or until thoroughly cooked. Top it with toppings of choice, reduce the heat to 350º F and bake the pizza for about15 minutes or until the toppings are cooked and the pizza is warm. Serve!

Makes 8 servings or one 14 inch pizza

✳ This recipe can be used to make whole grain buns for burgers. At step 3, instead of rolling out the dough into one large circle, divide the dough into 8 parts and roll the parts out into circles. Poke the circles with toothpicks before baking and bake only once at 400º F. Let the buns cool completely before slicing them in half.

✳ While you can top this pizza however you want, my favorite way to top this pizza crust is by slathering it with hummus, spooning on marinara sauce and then topping it with a mixture of sautéed mushrooms, garlic and onion as well as with Cashew Pizza Drizzle (p. 81). After baking it, I garnish it with parsley.

Nutrition Info
(per 1/8 recipe, 124g):

Calories: 276
Fat: 0g (0%)
Sodium: 148mg (6%)
Carbohydrates: 64g (21%)
Fiber: 9g (37%)
Sugars: 1g
Protein: 12g
Omega 3: .3mg
Thiamin: 2% (.0mg)
Riboflavin: 4% (.1mg)
Niacin: 2% (.4mg)
Folate: 7% (26.3mcg)
Iron: 19% (3.4mg)

{ I recommend **testing yeast before using it** if you don't frequently employ it. To test yeast, mix 1/2 cup warm water and 1 tbsp warm apple juice concentrate. To this mixture, add 2 1/4 tsp of yeast. If the yeast is good, the mixture will react and foam up. If the yeast is expired, it will not react when combined. }

Cashew Pizza Drizzle

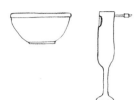

This simple dressing of cashew butter and olive oil is used in many of the pizza recipes in this chapter. It adds richness and flavor not only to pizza, but to pasta dishes and roasted vegetables too.

- **2 tbsp cashew butter**

- **2 - 4 tbsp olive oil**

- **Salt and black pepper to taste**

1. Using a handheld blender, blend the cashew butter and olive oil until smooth in a small mixing bowl. The mixture should have the thickness of a creamy salad dressing. Add more oil if needed and season to taste. Serve!

Makes 8 servings

(enough to top a 14 inch pizza or a pasta or vegetable dish serving 8)

 The amount of olive oil you will need depends on the thickness of your cashew butter. Some cashew butters become solid in the refrigerator while others stay very creamy.

 Flax option: Substitute flax oil for olive oil.

Nutritional Info
(per 1/8 serving, 9g):

Calories: 68
Fat: 7g (11%)
Sodium: 1mg (0%)
Carbohydrates: 1g (0%)
Protein: 1g
Omega 3: 821mg
VE: 4% (.7mg)
VK: 4% (3mcg)
Magnesium: 3% (10.3mg)
Phosphorus: 2% (18.3mg)
Copper: 4% (.0mg)
Manganese: 2% (.0mg)

Nutritional info is calculated with 3 tbsp of oil.

Lemony Potato Pizza

This yummy pizza uses slices of oven roasted potatoes for a crust. The potato crust is then garnished with veggies and a lemony cashew sauce to make a simple, healthy pizza that takes little time to prepare.

- **4 yellow potatoes, washed and halved lengthwise**
  (with rounded edges peeled off so the potato slice lays flat)

- **1 lemon slice**

- **Olive oil for brushing**

- **1 tsp Italian seasoning**

- **1 tsp olive oil**

- **1/2 onion, chopped**

- **1 clove garlic, minced**

- **3/4 cup sliced mushrooms**

- **1/4 tsp Italian seasoning**

- **1/2 recipe Cashew Pizza Drizzle (p. 81)**

- **1/2 tbsp cashew butter**

- **1 tbsp lemon juice**

- **1/2 cup marinara sauce**

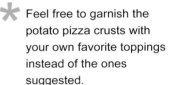

* Feel free to garnish the potato pizza crusts with your own favorite toppings instead of the ones suggested.

1. Preheat the oven to 400° F.

2. Place the potatoes cut-side down on an oiled baking tray. You should have 8 slices of potatoes in total. Rub the lemon slice on the cut-sides of the potatoes, brush them with oil, and sprinkle them with 1 tsp of the Italian seasoning. Bake the potatoes for 20 minutes in the preheated oven. Meanwhile, follow steps 3 and 4.

3. Heat olive oil in a skillet and sauté the onion, garlic, and mushrooms until tender. Stir in 1/4 tsp Italian seasoning. Set aside.

4. In a small bowl, use a handheld blender to combine the Cashew Pizza Drizzle, cashew butter, and lemon juice. Set aside.

5. Spoon about 1 tbsp marinara sauce onto each slice of potato. Top with the mushroom mixture (evenly divided among potatoes) and the lemon cashew sauce. Bake in the preheated oven for 10 minutes or until thoroughly cooked. Serve!

Makes 4 servings (2 slices of potato pizza = 1 serving)

Nutritional Info
(per 1/4 recipe, 229g):

Calories: 243
Fat: 8g (13%)
Sodium: 172mg (7%)
Carbohydrates: 39g (13%)
Fiber: 3g, Sugars: 5g
Protein: 5g
Omega 3: 66mg
VA: 2% (108IU)
VC: 42% (25mg)
VE: 6% (1.2mg)
VK: 6% (4.4mcg)
Thiamin: 14% (.2mg)
Riboflavin: 8% (.1mg)
Niacin: 16% (3.1mg)
B6: 27% (.5mg)
Folate: 7% (27.3mcg)
B5: 12% (1.2mg)
Calcium: 2% (19.7mg)
Iron: 7% (1.3mg)
Magnesium: 16% (62.6mg)
Phosphorus: 13% (133mg)
Potassium: 24% (825mg)
Zinc: 6% (.9mg)
Copper: 28% (.6mg)
Manganese: 18% (.4mg)
Selenium: 5% (3.3mcg)

Millet Cipolla Pizza

This pizza uses a risotto-like preparation of cooked millet, a nutritious whole grain, as a pizza crust and is topped with an onion (cipolla is the Italian word for onion) mixture.

For the crust:

- **1 cup dry millet (p. 17)**
- **2 cups vegetable broth**
- **1 tbsp cashew butter**
- **1 tbsp nutritional yeast**
- **1/2 tsp garlic powder**
- **1/2 tsp onion powder**

For the toppings:

- **1/2 tbsp olive oil**
- **3 onions, chopped**
- **2 cloves garlic, minced**
- **1/2 cup cooked chickpeas**
- **1/2 cup marinara sauce**
- **1/4 cup halved olives**
- **1 tbsp capers**
- **1/2 tsp Italian seasoning**
- **1 recipe Cashew Pizza Drizzle (p. 81)**

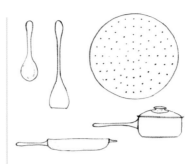

* Feel free to use another topping in place of the topping suggested.

❖ *Flax option: Stir 2 tbsp flax meal into millet mixture at step one.*

1. Preheat the oven to 350° F.

2. In a medium-sized pot, combine the millet, vegetable broth, cashew butter, nutritional yeast, and seasonings. Bring the mixture to a boil and then reduce the heat to low. Cook for about 20 minutes or until all the liquid is absorbed. Meanwhile, follow step 3.

3. Heat the oil in a skillet and sauté the onions and garlic for about 7 minutes or until tender. Stir in the chickpeas, marinara sauce, olives, capers, and Italian seasoning. Set aside.

4. Form the crust. Place the millet mixture on a 14 inch pizza pan lined with aluminium foil. Using a spatula (wrapped in aluminium foil to prevent sticking), firmly and evenly press the millet mixture into a thin layer that spreads across the pan. Top the pizza with the onion mixture and drizzle with Cashew Pizza Drizzle.

5. Bake pizza in preheated oven for about 15 minutes. Remove from oven and cut pizza into slices. Delicately handle slices while serving. Serve!

Makes 8 servings or one 14 inch pizza

Nutritional Info
(per 1/8 recipe, 171g):

Calories: 245
Fat: 11g (17%)
Sodium: 75mg (3%)
Carbohydrates: 31g (10%)
Fiber: 5g, Sugars: 4g
Protein: 7g
Omega 3: 97.8mg
VA: 3% (163IU)
VC: 10% (6mg)
VE: 6% (1.3mg)
VK: 7% (5.4mcg)
Thiamin: 82% (1.2mg)
Riboflavin: 69% (1.2mg)
Niacin: 39% (7.7mg)
B6: 64% (1.3mg)
Folate: 21% (85.4mcg)
B12: 15% (.9mcg)
B5: 5% (.5mg)
Calcium: 3% (30.3mg)
Iron: 11% (1.9mg)
Magnesium: 15% (60.9mg)
Phosphorus: 16% (160mg)
Potassium: 8% (281mg)
Zinc: 10% (1.4mg)
Copper: 22% (.4mg)
Manganese: 35% (.7mg)
Selenium: 7% (4.9mcg)

Lentil Vegetable Curry Soup (p. 91)

Simply Souper

Soup for supper? Of course! Easy to make and leaving you only with a soup pot and spoon to wash, soup is convenient. It makes the best leftovers and thanks to the thermos, it's portable. Plus- soup is naturally healthy, tasty, and appealing to everyone. The soups in this chapter are no exception and they are sure to please.

Chickpea Vegetable Soup

This is one of those simple soups that everyone loves. Since it uses vegetables that most people usually have on hand, this soup is ideal for quick dinners. Try serving it with warm, whole grain bread spread with Creamy Basic Hummus on p. 27 and steamed veggies for a yummy meal.

- **1/2 tbsp olive oil**
- **1 onion, chopped**
- **2 garlic cloves, minced**
- **1 cup chopped carrots**
- **1 cup chopped zucchini**
- **5 cups vegetable broth**
- **3 tbsp tomato paste**
- **1/4 cup dry whole grain pasta shells or small pasta shapes**

  ✿ *Gluten-free option: Use gluten-free whole grain pasta*

- **1 tsp dried basil**
- **1 tsp dried oregano**
- **1/4 tsp black pepper**
- **1 pinch ground thyme**
- **2 cups cooked chickpeas**

1. Heat the oil in a soup pot and then add the onion and garlic and sauté them for about 5 minutes. Add the carrots and zucchini and sauté for 2 more minutes.

2. Stir in the stock, tomato paste, and pasta. Bring the soup to a boil uncovered, then cover and reduce heat.

3. Simmer the soup for 8 to 10 minutes. Keep an eye on the pasta and vegetables; be careful not to overcook them. Add the seasonings and chickpeas. Serve!

Makes 6 servings

 If you wish, pinto beans, black-eyed peas, kidney beans or black beans can be substituted for chickpeas.

Nutritional Info
(1/6 recipe, 350g):

Calories: 213
Fat: 3g (5%)
Carbohydrates: 38g (13%)
Fiber: 9g, Sugars: 9g
Protein: 9g
Omega 3: 54.8 mg
VA: 92% (4615IU)
VC: 12% (7.2mg)
VE: 5% (1mg)
VK: 14% (13.7mcg)
Thiamin: 13% (.2mg)
Riboflavin: 6% (.1mg)
Niacin: 7% (1.5mg)
B6: 11% (.2mg)
Folate: 44% (178mcg)
B5: 3% (.3mg)
Calcium: 6% (63.4mg)
Iron: 18% (3.3mg)
Magnesium: 13% (51.4mg)
Phosphorus: 16% (159mg)
Potassium: 14% (480mg)
Zinc: 9% (1.4mg)
Copper: 17% (.3mg)
Manganese: 47% (.9mg)
Selenium: 5% (3.5mcg)

Coconut Curry Stew

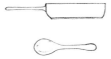

This curry-like dish is quick and easy to prepare and very tasty. Serve it over brown rice for a simple, nourishing meal.

- **2 tsp olive oil**

- **3 garlic cloves, minced**

- **1/2 onion, chopped**

- **1 green bell pepper, chopped**

- **2 cups cooked chickpeas**

- **28 oz can diced tomatoes**

- **1/4 cup coconut milk**

- **1 tsp curry powder**

- **Cayenne pepper to taste**

1. Heat the oil in a saucepan and gently sauté the onion and garlic for 5 to 7 minutes.

2. Add the chickpeas and green pepper and sauté for a few more minutes.

3. Add the tomatoes and simmer for about 10 minutes, uncovered. Stir in the coconut milk and seasonings. Serve!

Makes 4 servings

✳ If desired, a cup of frozen green peas can be used instead of the green bell pepper.

Nutritional Info
(per 1/4 serving 341g):

Calories: 232
Fat: 8g (12%)
Carbohydrates: 34g (11%)
Fiber: 9g, Sugars: 10g
Protein: 10g
Omega 3: 61.8mg
VA: 7% (367IU)
VC: 75% (45.1mg)
VE: 11% (2.2mg)
VK: 16% (13.1mg)
Thiamin: 14% (.2mg)
Riboflavin: 10% (.2mg)
Niacin: 11% (2.1mg)
B6: 23% (.5mg)
Folate: 41% (165mcg)
B5: 5% (.5mg)
Calcium: 12% (116mg)
Iron: 28% (5.1mg)
Magnesium: 18% (73.6mg)
Phosphorus: 20% (204mg)
Potassium: 21% (727mg)
Zinc: 11% (1.7mg)
Copper: 25% (.5mg)
Manganese: 61% (1.2mg)
Selenium: 5% (3.7mcg)

Curried Carrot Soup

This super quick, super easy soup is a tasty variety of carrot soup. Coconut milk and curry powder add flavor, but not time. Serve this soup with Fruit'n Nut Pilaf on p. 43 for a quick, light meal.

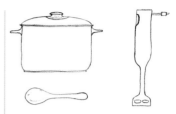

- 1/2 tbsp olive oil
- 1 onion, chopped
- 2 cups chopped carrots
- 2 cups cooked yellow split peas
- 3 1/2 cup vegetable broth
- 1 tsp curry powder
- 1/3 cup coconut milk
- 1 to 2 tbsp lemon juice

Carrots can be substituted by an equal amount of butternut squash

1. Heat the oil in soup pot and sauté onion for 5 minutes. Add the carrots and continue to sauté for a few more minutes.

2. Stir in the curry powder, yellow split peas, and vegetable broth. Bring to a boil, then lower the heat and simmer until the carrots are soft.

3. Remove the soup from the stove and puree the it until smooth using a handheld blender.

4. Add the coconut milk and lemon juice and heat thoroughly. Serve!

Makes 4 servings

Nutritional Info
(per 1/4 recipe, 341g):

Calories: 102
Fat: 6g (9%)
Carbohydrates: 13g (4%)
Fiber: 2g, Sugars: 6g
Protein: 1g
VA: 219% (10959IU)
VC: 18% (10.8mg)
VE: 4% (.8mg)
VK: 13% (10.1mcg)
Thiamin: 4% (.1mg)
Riboflavin: 3% (.0mg)
Niacin: 4% (.8mg)
B6: 7% (.1mg)
Folate: 5% (165mcg)
B5: 2% (.2mg)
Calcium: 3% (47.7mg)
Iron: 5% (1mg)
Magnesium: 5% (19.9mg)
Phosphorus: 5% (48.8mg)
Potassium: 9% (299mg)
Zinc: 2% (.3mg)
Copper: 4% (.1mg)
Manganese: 14% (.3mg)

Creamy Coconut Tomato Soup

This savory soup is simple to make and uses most of the tomato without compromising taste. This recipe uses a few unusual cooking methods to save time. Serve with toasted whole grain bread spread with Creamy Basic Hummus on p. 27, Lovely Lentil Salad on p. 46, and steamed veggies, like spinach or broccoli.

- **6 medium tomatoes, chopped**

- **1 1/2 cup vegetable juice**

- **1/4 tsp cumin**

- **1 tsp dried basil**

- **Salt and pepper to taste**

- **1/3 cup coconut milk**

1. Place the tomatoes in a large mixing bowl and puree them until smooth using a handheld blender.

2. Now, pass the tomato mixture through a sieve over a soup pot. Discard the sieve remains.

3. Add the vegetable juice to the tomato mixture and bring to a boil. Stir in the seasonings and coconut milk and reduce the heat. Let the soup simmer, partially covered, for 15 to 20 minutes. Serve!

Makes 4 servings

✳ If you can, use 1 tbsp fresh basil in this soup rather than the dried basil.

Nutritional Info
(per 1/4 serving 291g):

Calories: 96
Fat: 5g (8%)
Carbohydrates: 12g (4%)
Fiber: 3g, Sugars: 8g
Protein: 3g
Omega 3: 13.3mg
VA: 46% (2277IU)
VC: 57% (34.2mg)
VE: 5% (1mg)
VK: 29% (23.2mcg)
Thiamin: 5% (.1mg)
Riboflavin: 2% (.0mg)
Niacin: 6% (1.3mg)
B6: 8% (.2mg)
Folate: 8% (32.2mcg)
B5: 2% (.2mg)
Calcium: 5% (47.7mg)
Iron: 10% (1.8mg)
Magnesium: 8% (33.2mg)
Phosphorus: 7% (69mg)
Potassium: 19% (668mg)
Zinc: 3% (.5mg)
Copper: 8% (.2mg)
Manganese: 20% (.4mg)

Ginger Vegetable Soup

This spicy, gingery, vegetable soup is full of flavor. Enjoy it with Sweet Potato Fries on p. 40 as well as with some whole grain bread spread with Creamy Basic Hummus on p. 27.

- **1/4 cup freshly grated ginger**
- **4 cups vegetable broth**
- **1/2 tbsp sesame oil**
- **2 garlic cloves, minced**
- **1 onion, chopped**
- **1 cup chopped carrots**
- **1 cup broccoli florets**
- **3 tbsp tomato paste**
- **2 cups cooked black beans**
- **1 tbsp soy sauce**
- **1 tbsp fresh parsley**

1. Mix the vegetable broth and ginger in a medium-sized pot and bring to a boil. Let boil for 15 minutes and set aside.

2. Heat the oil in a soup pot. Fry the onion and garlic for about 5 minutes. Add the carrots and cook for 3 more minutes. Add the broccoli and sauté for another 3 minutes.

3. Add the ginger broth, tomato paste, black beans, and soy sauce. Bring to a boil and simmer for about 15 minutes or until the vegetables are tender. Stir in the parsley. Serve!

Makes 4 servings

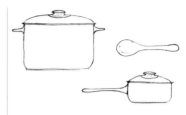

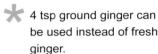

* 4 tsp ground ginger can be used instead of fresh ginger.

* Cooked red kidney beans can be used instead of black beans.

Nutritional Info
(per 1/4 recipe, 432g):

Calories: 196
Fat: 3g (4%)
Carbohydrates: 35g (12%)
Fiber: 9g, Sugars: 5g
Protein: 10g
Omega 3: 209mg
VA: 125% (6249IU)
VC: 55% (33.3mg)
VE: 4% (.9mg)
VK: 84% (67.1mcg)
Thiamin: 14% (.2mg)
Riboflavin: 8% (.1mg)
Niacin: 7% (1.4mg)
B6: 16% (.3mg)
Folate: 43% (171mcg)
B5: 6% (.6mg)
Calcium: 7% (69.3mg)
Iron: 14% (2.6mg)
Magnesium: 15% (60.1mg)
Phosphorus: 18% (180mg)
Potassium: 20% (689mg)
Zinc: 8% (1.3mg)
Copper: 14% (.3mg)
Manganese: 31% (.6mg)
Selenium: 3% (2.1mcg)

Lentil Vegetable Curry Soup

This vegetable-filled soup is a good, wholesome choice for quick dinners with its filling lentils and vitamin rich vegetables.

- **1 tbsp olive oil**
- **1 onion, chopped**
- **2 garlic cloves, minced**
- **6 cups vegetable broth**
- **1 1/2 cup frozen green peas**
- **1 cup dry green lentils**
- **28 oz can tomatoes**
- **1 1/2 tsp curry powder**
- **1 tsp soy sauce**
- **1/8 tsp dried oregano**
- **Ground thyme, cayenne and black pepper, and salt to taste**
- **1 1/2 cup shredded carrots**

1. In a soup pot, heat the oil. Sauté the onion and garlic for about 5 minutes.

2. Add the broth, peas, lentils, and tomatoes. Bring the soup to a boil. Simmer for about 20 minutes or until the lentils and peas are cooked.

3. Stir in the seasonings and carrots (The heat from soup should be enough to cook carrots.). Serve!

Makes 8 servings

 Substitute cooked chickpeas, black-eyed peas or black beans for lentils.

Nutritional Info
(per 1/8 recipe, 353g):

Calories: 150
Fat: 1g (2%)
Carbohydrates: 28g (9%)
Fiber: 10g, Sugars: 7g
Protein: 9g
Omega 3: 40.2 mg
VA: 87% (4354IU)
VC: 31% (18.9mg)
VE: 5% (1mg)
VK: 17% (13.7mcg)
Thiamin: 23% (.3mg)
Riboflavin: 9% (.2mg)
Niacin: 10% (2.1mg)
B6: 17% (.3mg)
Folate: 36% (144mcg)
B5: 7% (.3mg)
Calcium: 6% (63.3mg)
Iron: 19% (3.4mg)
Magnesium: 13% (52.1mg)
Phosphorus: 16% (163mg)
Potassium: 16% (550mg)
Zinc: 11% (1.6mg)
Copper: 12% (.2mg)
Manganese: 28% (.6mg)
Selenium: 4% (2.8mcg)

Mushroom Pinto Bean Soup

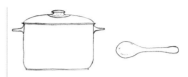

This warm, savory soup has a wonderful flavor. It can be served with French bread and a side salad to make a nice dinner.

- **1 tbsp olive oil**
- **1 onion, chopped**
- **2 garlic cloves, minced**
- **2 cups sliced mushrooms**
- **2 1/2 cups cooked pinto beans**
- **4 cups vegetable broth**
- **1/2 tsp soy sauce**

- **1 tbsp sherry (optional)**
- **1/2 cup dry brown rice**
- **3/4 tsp dried rosemary**
- **3/4 tsp dried parsley**
- **1/2 red bell pepper, roasted (p. 18) and chopped**
- **Salt and black pepper to taste**

1. In a soup pot, heat the oil until hot then add onion and garlic. Sauté for about 5 minutes. Add the mushrooms and sauté for a few more minutes.

2. Add the vegetable broth, pinto beans, sherry, soy sauce, and rice. Bring the mixture to a boil, uncovered. Reduce the heat and simmer until rice is cooked, about 20 minutes.

3. Once rice is cooked, add the seasonings and roasted pepper. Serve!

Makes 4 servings

✳ If you want to make sure the alcohol (sherry) is completely cooked off, let the soup boil for a few minutes extra or leave it out altogether.

Nutritional info
(1/4 recipe, 469g):

Calories: 257
Fat: 1g (2%)
Carbohydrates: 49 g (16%)
Fiber: 13g, Sugars: 5g
Protein: 13g
Omega 3: 159mg
VA: 19% (957IU)
VC: 24% (14.6mg)
VD: 3% (11.3IU)
VE: 6% (1.2mg)
VK: 7% (5.9mcg)
Thiamin: 22% (.3mg)
Riboflavin: 20% (.3mg)
Niacin: 17% (3.4mg)
B6: 21% (.4mg)
Folate: 51% (205mcg)
B5: 12% (1.2mg)
Calcium: 7% (68.6mg)
Iron: 16% (2.9mg)
Magnesium: 21% (85.4mg)
Phosphorus: 27% (269mg)
Potassium: 22% (772mg)
Zinc: 12% (1.8mg)
Copper: 23% (.5mg)
Manganese: 52% (1mg)
Selenium: 28% (19.3mcg)

Refreshing Rainbow Stew

This thick stew is chock-full of good-for-you veggies. Serve it with Sweet Potato Fries on p. 40 and steamed veggies.

- **28 oz can chopped tomatoes**
- **1 1/4 cup vegetable broth**
- **2 cups cooked black beans**
- **1 onion, chopped**
- **1 rutabaga, peeled and chopped into small cubes**
- **2 cups collard greens, chopped and de-stemmed**
- **1 tsp chili powder**
- **1 tsp curry powder**
- **1 tsp celery seed**
- **Dried oregano to taste**
- **Olive oil for drizzling**

1. Combine the tomatoes, broth, beans, onion, and rutabaga in a soup pot.

2. Bring to a boil then reduce heat and let the stew simmer.

3. Cook for about 25 minutes or until all the vegetables are tender. Now stir in the collard greens and seasonings. Wait for collard greens to wilt. Drizzle individual servings with olive oil. Serve!

Makes 4 servings

 Collard greens are nutritious, green, leafy vegetables that are available at some grocery stores or supermarkets, depending on where you live. If you have trouble finding collard greens, you can replace them with kale or spinach.

 Flax option: Use flax oil for drizzling rather than olive oil.

Nutritional Info
(per 1/4 recipe, 496g):

Calories: 208
Fat: 1g (2%)
Carbohydrates: 41g (14%)
Fiber: 13g, Sugars: 12g
Protein: 11g
Omega 3: 174mg
VA: 34% (1721IU)
VC: 86% (51.8mg)
VE: 12% (2.3mg)
VK: 124% (99.2mcg)
Thiamin: 27% (.4mg)
Riboflavin: 14% (.2mg)
Niacin: 14% (2.8mg)
B6: 23% (.5mg)
Folate: 50% (201mcg)
B5: 7% (.7mg)
Calcium: 17% (175mg)
Iron: 26% (4.8mg)
Magnesium: 28% (113mg)
Phosphorus: 23% (230mg)
Potassium: 31% (1096mg)
Zinc: 11% (1.7mg)
Copper: 19% (.4mg)
Manganese: 43% (.9mg)
Selenium: 4% (2.5mcg)

Sneaky Butternut Lentil Soup

This is one sneaky soup, hidden among its creaminess and cinnamon undertones are good-for-you squash and lentils. Try serving it with a salad of greens and a bean burger of your choice.

- **1/2 tbsp olive oil**
- **1 onion, chopped**
- **2 medium apples, chopped**
- **3 cups vegetable broth**
- **1 cup water**
- **2 tbsp apple juice concentrate**
- **1 cup dry red lentils**
- **1 cup plain almond milk**
- **2 cups cooked butternut squash**
- **1/2 tsp cinnamon**
- **Pinch nutmeg and ground ginger**

1. Heat the oil in a soup pot and gently fry the apples and onion for 5 minutes.

2. Add the vegetable broth, water, juice, lentils, and squash.

3. Bring to a boil and simmer for 20 to 30 minutes or until the apples, onion, and lentils are cooked.

4. Add the almond milk and seasonings and then puree the soup until smooth using a handheld blender. Heat the soup until desired temperature is reached. Serve!

Makes 6 servings

 I prefer to cook large amounts of butternut squash in the oven and use it to prepare several different recipes, such as Autumnal Vegetable Pasta Sauce on p. 69. For directions about cooking butternut squash, see p. 14.

 To make your own almond milk, mix 1 cup water with 1/4 cup almonds, ground into a flour.

Nutritional Info
(1/6 recipe, 373g):

Calories: 234
Fat: 5g (7%)
Carbohydrates: 40g (13%)
Fiber: 13g
Sugars: 11g
Protein: 11g
Omega 3: 66.4mg
VA: 160% (7995IU)
VC: 26% (15.9mg)
VE: 24% (2.9mg)
VK: 6% (4.4mcg)
Thiamin: 24% (.4mg)
Riboflavin: 9% (.2mg)
Niacin: 9% (1.8mg)
B6: 16% (.3mg)
Folate: 44% (175mcg)
B5: 10% (1mg)
Calcium: 7% (73.9mg)
Iron: 18% (3.2mg)
Magnesium: 20% (80.6mg)
Phosphorus: 20% (204mg)
Potassium: 18% (1634mg)
Zinc: 12% (1.9mg)
Copper: 15% (.3mg)
Manganese: 38% (.8mg)
Selenium: 5% (3.2mcg)

Vegetable Black-Eyed Pea Soup

This soup is stuffed with wholesome and healthy veggies that will ensure you get your daily vegetable quota. Serve with cooked brown rice.

- **1/2 tbsp olive oil**
- **1 onion, chopped**
- **2 cups chopped celery**
- **2 garlic cloves, minced**
- **6 1/2 cups vegetable broth**
- **1/3 cup tomato paste**
- **1 cup shredded rutabaga**
- **1 cup shredded carrots**
- **2 cups cooked black-eyed peas**
- **3/4 tsp paprika**
- **1/2 tsp dried thyme**
- **1 tsp dried oregano**

1. Heat the oil in a soup pot and sauté the onion, celery, and garlic for about 5 minutes.

2. Stir in the vegetable broth and tomato paste. Bring the soup to a boil, reduce the heat, and simmer for 10 to 15 minutes or until the onion and celery are fork tender.

3. Stir in the rutabaga, carrots, seasonings, and beans. Simmer until warm. Serve!

Makes 8 servings

 Fresh herbs are wonderful in this soup. If you have some on hand, you can substitute 1 tbsp of fresh oregano and thyme for the dried thyme and oregano.

Nutritional Info
(per 1/8 recipe, 326g):

Calories: 120
Fat: 1g (2%)
Carbohydrates: 22g (7%)
Fiber: 6g
Sugars: 7g
Protein: 6g
Omega 3: 27.7mg
VA: 59% (2947IU)
VC: 20% (11.9mg)
VE: 5% (1mg)
VK: 17% (13.2mcg)
Thiamin: 3% (.0mg)
Riboflavin: 3% (.1mg)
Niacin: 4% (.8mg)
B6: 6% (.1mg)
Folate: 5% (19.7mcg)
B5: 2% (.2mg)
Calcium: 4% (40.4mg)
Iron: 12% (2.1mg)
Magnesium: 4% (16.7mg)
Phosphorus: 4% (38.9mg)
Potassium: 9% (331mg)
Zinc: 2% (.3mg)
Copper: 4% (.1mg)
Manganese: 8% (.2mg)
Selenium: 2% (1.1mcg)

Vegetable Sunshine Soup

Sun-dried tomatoes give this soup flavor and punch, thus the name "sunshine". This soup is great served with croutons (see p. 20 to learn how to make your own).

- **1 tbsp olive oil**
- **1 onion, chopped**
- **2 medium garlic clove, minced**
- **1 1/2 cup carrots, chopped**
- **1 1/2 cup chopped asparagus**
- **10 sun-dried tomatoes (in oil), chopped**
- **2 cups cooked chickpeas**
- **5 1/2 cups vegetable broth**
- **1/2 tsp dried basil**
- **1/2 tsp dried oregano**

1. Heat the oil in a soup pot and sauté the onion and garlic for 5 minutes. Add the carrots and asparagus and cook for 3 to 5 minutes further.

2. Add the tomatoes, chickpeas, broth, seasonings, and bring to a boil.

3. Let simmer for 10 to 15 minutes or until the vegetables are cooked. Serve!

Makes 6 servings

 I prefer to use sun-dried tomatoes packed in oil for all my recipes because I find they have a better flavor compared to air-packed sun-dried tomatoes.

Nutritional Info
(1/6 of recipe, 352g):

Calories: 163
Fat: 5g (7%)
Carbohydrates: 25g: (8%)
Fiber: 6g, Sugars: 7g
Protein: 6g
Omega 3: 53.6mg
VA: 119% (5962IU)
VC: 22% (12.9mg)
VE: 6% (1.1mg)
VK: 29% (23mg)
Thiamin: 10% (.2mg)
Riboflavin: 7% (.1mg)
Niacin: 6% (1.1mg)
B6: 10% (.2mg)
Folate: 31% (123mcg)
B5: 4% (.4mg)
Calcium: 6% (56mg)
Iron: 15% (2.6mg)
Magnesium: 10% (41.3mg)
Phosphorus: 13% (135mg)
Potassium: 13% (441mg)
Zinc: 8% (1.2mg)
Copper: 15% (.3mg)
Manganese: 37% (.7mg)
Selenium: 5% (3.2mcg)

Wild Sun Stew

This cheerful mixture of wild rice, sunflower seeds, tomatoes, and sweet potato makes this chili a hearty, filling meal. Serve it with whole grain bread and cooked green peas or a green salad.

- **28 oz can diced tomatoes**

- **1/2 cup wild rice mix**

- **1 medium sweet potato, chopped into small cubes**

- **2 cups cooked chickpeas**

- **1 3/4 cup vegetable broth or water**

- **1 bay leaf**

- **1/2 tsp dried basil**

- **Cumin, ground thyme, and black pepper to taste**

- **1/3 cup roasted, salted sunflower seeds or roasted pecans**

- **Olive oil for drizzling**

1. Mix the tomatoes, rice, potatoes, broth, and seasonings in a soup pot. Bring the mixture to a boil uncovered, then let simmer partially covered for 20 minutes or until the rice and potato are cooked.

2. Stir in the sunflower seeds and remove the bay leaf. Serve!

Makes 4 servings

 Wild rice mix is a blend of wild rice, long grain brown rice, and basmati rice. You can find it at large supermarkets next to other rice products. Alternatively, combine 1 part wild rice with 1 part brown rice.

 Flax option: Flax oil can be used instead of olive oil for drizzling.

Nutritional Info
(per 1/4 serving, 438g):

Calories: 327
Fat: 5g (8%)
Carbohydrates: 61g (20%)
Fiber: 13g, Sugars: 7g
Protein: 15g
Omega 3: 109mg
VA: 149% (7471IU)
VC: 42% (24.9mg)
VE: 10% (2mg)
VK: 6% (4.5mcg)
Thiamin: 23% (.3mg)
Riboflavin: 14% (.2mg)
Niacin: 23% (4.7mg)
B6: 30% (.6mg)
Folate: 49% (196mcg)
B5: 13% (1.3mg)
Calcium: 14% (138mg)
Iron: 34% (6.1mg)
Magnesium: 34% (136mg)
Phosphorus: 33% (326mg)
Potassium: 29% (1019mg)
Zinc: 22% (3.3mg)
Copper: 43% (.9mg)
Manganese: 85% (1.7mg)
Selenium: 10% (6.8mcg)

Desserts

Vanilla and Peanut Carob Swirl Muffins (p. 109)

Cranberry Apricot Cookies (p. 104)

Brownies (p. 103)

Baked Goodies

Muffins, cakes, and brownies, oh my! Healthy desserts are nothing to be afraid of they aren't fussy and they taste great. In this chapter, you'll find recipes for healthful baked goods that are made with whole grains and sweetened with fruit. But remember, just because these desserts are healthier than most does not mean you can use them as a substitute for healthy meals and snacks. To reap the benefits of eating a healthy dessert, you must eat it for dessert.

Healthy Baking: Q & A

What is the difference between whole wheat pastry flour and whole wheat flour?

Whole wheat pastry flour, also known as white whole wheat flour, is made from a softer variety of wheat than regular whole wheat flour which allows it to produce baked goods with a lighter crumb than regular whole wheat flour. It is preferable to use whole wheat pastry flour in baking and not substitute it with whole wheat flour.

How can I make healthy baked goods with spelt flour?

In all of my baked good recipes, I give spelt options. There are many advantages to cooking with spelt, including added nutrition, moister baked goods, and a superior taste, however spelt flour is not widely available, so while I keep the option open, it is not necessary to use spelt for any of the recipes in this chapter. As a general rule, when substituting spelt flour for whole wheat pastry flour, use 1 cup + 2 tbsp spelt and 1/8 tsp extra baking powder and baking soda each as a substitute to 1 cup whole wheat pastry flour.

What is the purpose of nut butter in baked goods?

In the following baked good recipes, nut butter is used not only to flavor baked goods, but also to replace eggs and oil, making it an ingredient that cannot be omitted or replaced. If allergies are a concern, nut butters can be replaced with a different seed or nut butter then the one called for in a recipe.

What is the purpose of salt in baked goods?

Salt not only helps baked goods to rise, it helps to make the flavors of the baked good harmonize and become more distinct. It is not an optional ingredient and cannot be left out. Iodized salt or sea salt can be used.

What about apple juice concentrate? Can it be substituted?

Apple juice concentrate is used to sweeten healthful baked goods made without sugar. If desired, it can be substituted by a liquid sweetener such as maple syrup or honey, although the amount of liquid in the recipe will have to be increased and the seasonings may have to be adjusted.

What does it mean to "fluff" the batter?

Fluff- incorporate air into the batter by very gently folding it over itself.

* In order to make sure that your baked goods are successful, you'll need to know if your oven temperature is correct. An oven that is too hot or too cool can have negative effects on baked goods (make them sink, make them undercooked, etc.). Many oven thermometers are off, so if you suspect yours is, you may want to invest in a separate thermometer to indicate your oven's true temperature.

Brownies

This recipe for brownies is full of healthy foods such as flax, walnuts, whole grain flour, dates, and cashew butter.

- **1 cup carob chips or semi-sweet chocolate chips**

- **1/4 cup cashew butter**

- **1/4 cup flax meal mixed with**

- **1/3 cup apple juice concentrate**

- **1/3 cup date puree**

- **1 cup whole wheat pastry flour**

  ★ *Spelt option:* Use 1 cup + 2 tbsp spelt flour and 1/4 tsp extra baking powder

- **1/3 cup chopped walnuts**

- **1/2 tsp vanilla extract**

- **1/2 tsp baking powder**

- **1/4 tsp salt**

- **Coconut flour for dusting (optional)**

1. Preheat the oven to 375 °F.

2. In a mixing bowl, mix flour, baking powder, and salt.

3. In a small pot, slowly melt the carob and the cashew butter over very low heat.

4. Transfer the melted carob mixture to a small mixing bowl and stir in flax seed mixture, vanilla extract, and date puree. Make sure the flax seed mixture and date puree are warm or at room temperature to make mixing the ingredients easier and to prevent the carob/chocolate from hardening.

5. Mix carob mixture into dry ingredients, being careful not to overmix it. Fold in walnuts.

6. Pour carob mixture into an oiled 8 x 8 pan and carefully and evenly spread it out. The mixture should just fill the bottom of the pan. Bake the brownies in a preheated oven for 25 to 35 minutes or until a fork comes out clean. Let cool, then cut into squares. Dust with coconut flour. Serve!

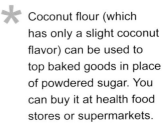

* Coconut flour (which has only a slight coconut flavor) can be used to top baked goods in place of powdered sugar. You can buy it at health food stores or supermarkets.

Nutritional Info
(per 1/16 recipe, 42g):

Calories: 173, Fat: 8g (12%)
Sodium: 54mg (2%)
Carbohydrates: 26g (9%)
Fiber: 3g, Sugars: 8g
Protein: 4g
Omega 3: 606mg
B6: 2% (.0mg)
Calcium: 3% (32.8mg)
Iron: 5% (.9mg)
Magnesium: 4% (15.8mg)
Phosphorus: 3% (31.8mg)
Potassium: 2% (70.2mg)
Zinc: 2% (.3mg)
Copper: 7% (.1mg)
Manganese: 6% (.1mg)

Makes 16 brownies

Cranberry Apricot Cookies

These scrumptious cookies are sweet, tender, and flavorful. Millet adds flavor and crunch while apricot puree keeps these cookies moist but still crispy.

- **1 cup whole wheat pastry flour**

  ★ *Spelt option: Use 1 1/4 cup + 1 tbsp spelt flour*

- **1/2 tsp salt**

- **1/2 tsp baking soda**

- **1/3 cup dried cranberries**

- **2 tbsp dry millet**

- **1/2 tsp lemon zest**

- **1/4 tsp ground ginger**

- **Pinch cinnamon**

- **3/4 cup apricot puree**

- **1/4 cup canola oil**

1. Preheat the oven to 375° F.

2. In a medium-sized mixing bowl, mix flour, baking soda, salt, cranberries, millet, zest, and seasonings. Add apricot puree and oil and thoroughly combine.

3. Using 2 tbsp (1 oz) of cookie dough for each cookie, roll all the portions of cookie dough into a ball and then flatten them into disks on a baking tray lined with parchment paper. Keep in mind that these cookies don't melt while baking, so they need to be flattened out and formed accordingly.

4. Bake the cookies for about 17 minutes in the preheated oven or until they are lightly browned on top, but still tender. Remove from oven and let cool before removing from baking tray. Serve!

Makes about twelve 1 oz cookies

★ To make apricot puree, place a cup of apricots in a small pot and cover with water. Bring to a boil over high heat. Let simmer until apricots are tender and most of the water has been absorbed. Puree until smooth using a handheld blender. This yields about a cup of puree.

Nutritional Info
(per cookie, 46g):

Calories: 108
Fat: 5g (8%)
Sodium: 150mg (6%)
Carbohydrates: 16g (5%)
Fiber: 2g
Sugars: 6g
Protein: 2g
Omega 3: 433mg
VA: 5% (267IU)
VE: 6% (1.3mg)
VK: 5% (3.9mcg)
Thiamin: 3% (.1mg)
Riboflavin: 2% (.0mg)
Iron: 4% (.6mg)
Magnesium: 4% (17.7mg)
Potassium: 4% (131mg)
Zinc: 2% (.3mg)
Copper: 4% (.1mg)
Manganese: 22% (.4mg)
Selenium: 10% (7.3mcg)

Charming Carrot Cake

This version of carrot cake is delicious! It's charming as no one can get enough of its yummy taste. It can be frosted with the cashew version of Almondy Carob Fruit Dip on p. 26.

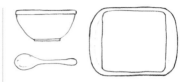

- **2 cups whole wheat pastry flour**

  ⭐ *Spelt option: Use 2 1/4 cups spelt flour and an extra 1/4 tsp baking powder and 1/4 tsp baking soda*

- **1/2 cup rolled oats**

- **2 tsp baking soda**

- **2 tsp baking powder**

- **3/4 tsp salt**

- **1 tsp cinnamon**

- **1/3 cup chopped walnuts**

- **1/3 cup raisins**

- **1 2/3 cup apple juice concentrate**

- **1/4 cup cashew butter**

- **1/2 tsp vanilla extract**

- **2 cups shredded carrots**

1. Preheat the oven to 325° F.

2. In the a medium-sized mixing bowl, mix flour, oats, baking soda, and powder, salt, cinnamon, walnuts, and raisins.

3. In a separate mixing bowl, combine juice, cashew butter, and vanilla extract using a handheld blender.

4. Pour the juice mixture into the flour mixture and stir until combined, and then mix in carrots. "Fluff" batter.

5. Pour the cake batter into an oiled 8 x 8 pan. Bake the cake in the preheated oven for about 1 hour or until a toothpick comes out clean. Let cool slightly before serving and frosting. Serve!

Makes 16 servings

* If desired, stir in 1/3 cup finely chopped pineapple at step 4.

❖ *Flax option: Stir in 2-3 tbsp flax meal at step 2.*

Nutritional Info
(per 1/16, 67g):

Calories: 155
Fat: 4g (6%)
Sodium: 340mg (14%)
Carbohydrates: 28g (9%)
Fiber: 3g, Sugars: 12g
Protein: 4g
Omega 3: 219mg
VA: 46% (2299IU)
VC: 2% (1.4mg)
VK: 3% (2.4mcg)
Thiamin: 8% (.1mg)
Riboflavin: 4% (.1mg)
Niacin: 6% (1.3mg)
B6: 6% (.1mg)
Folate: 4% (15.3mcg)
B5: 3% (.3mg)
Calcium: 6% (56mg)
Iron: 8% (1.4mg)
Magnesium: 11% (45mg)
Phosphorus: 11% (115mg)
Potassium: 8% (279mg)
Zinc: 6% (.9mg)
Copper: 11% (.2mg)
Manganese: 44% (.9mg)
Selenium: 17% (12mcg)

Lemon Spice Cake

This lemon flavored cake is filled with a pudding-like frosting. Serve it with fresh fruit and herbal tea for an afternoon dessert.

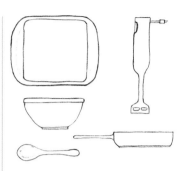

- **2 cups whole wheat pastry flour**

  ★ *Spelt option: Use 2 1/4 cups spelt flour and an extra1/4 tsp baking soda and 1/4 tsp baking powder.*

- **1 tsp baking soda**

- **1 tsp baking powder**

- **1/2 tsp salt**

- **1 tbsp lemon zest**

- **1/2 tsp cinnamon**

- **1/2 tsp ground ginger**

- **Nutmeg and ground cloves to taste**

- **1 cup apple juice concentrate**

- **1/2 cup lemon juice**

- **1/4 cup cashew butter**

- **1 cup cashews, ground into flour**

- **1 tsp lemon zest**

- **1/4 cup apple juice concentrate**

- **1/2 cup rice milk or other milk**

- **1 tbsp flour**

Nutritional Info
(per 1/16 of recipe, 92g):

Calories: 280
Fat: 15g (23%)
Sodium: 217mg (9%)
Carbohydrates: 33g (11%)
Fiber: 3g, Sugars: 10g
Protein: 8g
Omega 3: 34.4mg
VC: 7% (4.2mg)
VE: 2% (.4mg)
VK: 12% (9.9mcg)
Thiamin: 14% (.2mg)
Riboflavin: 4% (.1mg)
Niacin: 7% (1.5mg)
B6: 10% (.2mg)
Folate: 5% (2mcg)
B5: 5% (.5mg)
Calcium: 5% (46.4mg)
Iron: 17% (3mg)
Magnesium: 29% (117mg)
Phosphorus: 26% (259mg)
Potassium: 11% (374mg)
Zinc: 15% (2.3mg)
Copper: 39% (.8mg)
Manganese: 58% (1.2mg)
Selenium: 24% (17.4mcg)

1. Preheat the oven to 350° F.

2. In a medium-sized mixing bowl, mix the flour, baking soda, baking powder, salt, lemon zest, cinnamon, ginger, nutmeg and cloves.

3. In a separate, mixing bowl, combine 1 cup apple juice, 1/2 cup lemon juice and the cashew butter using a handheld blender.

4. Slowly incorporate the wet ingredients into the dry ones. 'Fluff' the batter, and then pour it into an oiled 8 x 8 pan. Bake in the preheated oven for about 35 minutes or until toothpick comes out clean.

5. Meanwhile, in a saucepan, whisk together the cashew flour, juice, rice milk, zest, and flour. Heat the mixture in a saucepan over medium heat until thickened, whisking and stirring continuously to prevent lumps.

6. Remove the cake from the baking pan and slice it in half horizontally. Spread the cashew mixture on cut-side of bottom piece of cake. Sandwich it with the other slice of cake. Serve!

Makes 16 servings

Peanut Carob Swirl Muffins

These delicious, decadent muffins have a great, rich, flavorful taste. Frost them with Almondy Carob Dip *(p. 26)* made with peanut butter instead of almond butter.

- **2 cups whole wheat pastry flour**

  ★ *Spelt option: Use 2 1/4 cups spelt flour and an extra 1/4 tsp baking soda and 1/4 tsp baking powder*

- **1 tsp baking soda**

- **1 tsp baking powder**

- **1/2 tsp salt**

- **1/2 cup creamy peanut butter**

- **1/2 cup rice milk or other milk**

- **1 1/2 cup apple juice concentrate**

- **1/2 tsp vanilla extract**

- **1/2 cup carob chips or semi-sweet chocolate chips**

1. Preheat the oven to 375° F.

2. In a small pot, melt the carob chips over low heat. Meanwhile, continue with the following steps.

3. In a medium-sized mixing bowl, mix the flour, baking soda, baking powder, and salt.

4. In a smaller bowl, use a handheld blender to blend the peanut butter, rice milk, juice, and vanilla extract.

5. Add the peanut butter mixture to the dry ingredients and combine, keeping stirring to a minimum. Remove 1 cup of this combined mixture, place it in a different mixing bowl, and stir in the melted carob chips.

6. Line a muffin tin with 12 baking cups. Pour equal amounts of half of the peanut butter batter into the bottoms of the cups, then add the carob mixture, and top with the remainder of peanut butter batter. Using a table knife, "swirl" the muffins by inserting the knife into the muffin batter and stirring.

7. Bake muffins in the preheated oven for about 15 minutes or until a toothpick comes out clean. Remove from the tin and let cool. Serve!

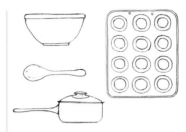

★ You can also make a cake using this recipe. At step 6, pour the batter into an oiled 8 x 8 pan, following the directions for swirling. Bake the cake for about 35 minutes or until a toothpick comes out clean at 375 degrees.

Nutritional Info
(per 1/12 recipe, 100g):

Calories: 281
Fat: 8g (13%)
Sodium: 253mg (11%)
Carbohydrates: 49g (16%)
Fiber: 5g
Sugars: 15g
Protein: 9g
Omega 3: 13.5mg
VE: 5% (1mg)
Riboflavin: 2% (.0mg)
Niacin: 7% (1.5mg)
B6: 5% (.1mg)
Folate: 2% (8.2mcg)
B5: 2% (.2mg)
Calcium: 5% (45.9mg)
Iron: 11% (1.9mg)
Magnesium: 5% (21.4mg)
Phosphorus: 5% (53.7mg)
Potassium: 6% (196mg)
Zinc: 2% (.3mg)
Copper: 3% (.1mg)
Manganese: 11% (.2mg)

Makes 12 muffins

Pretty Pecan Pie

This lovely pie has a sweet, creamy filling surrounded by a tasty, cookie-like crust. Despite the seemingly time consuming steps, this pie whips together like magic and tastes divine, so don't pass this one by in favor of a simpler recipe.

For the filling:

- **1 cup water**
- **1 tbsp flax seeds**
- **1/2 cup pecan butter or almond butter**
- **1/2 cup date puree**
- **1/2 cup apple juice**
- **1/4 cup rice milk or other milk**
- **1 tsp lemon juice**
- **1/2 tsp vanilla extract**

For the crust:

- **2 cups oats**
- **1/4 cup raw cashews**
- **1/2 tsp almond extract**
- **1 tsp cinnamon**
- **1/2 tbsp carob powder**
- **1/2 tsp lemon zest**
- **1/3 cup apple juice concentrate**

For the topping

- **Pecans, to top**

* If you wish, you can substitute a more traditional pie crust for the cookie-like crust, but make sure to choose a crust free of hydrogenated oils.

Nutritional Info (per 1/8 recipe, 112g):

Calories: 288
Fat: 14g (22%)
Sodium: 14mg (1%)
Carbohydrates: 37g (12%)
Fiber: 4g
Sugars: 15g
Protein: 7g
Omega 3: 387mg
VC: 2% (.9mg)
VK: 4% (3.2mcg)
Thiamin: 11% (.2mg)
Riboflavin: 9% (.2mg)
Niacin: 5% (1mg)
B6: 5% (.1mg)
Folate: 5% (21.7mcg)
B5: 4% (.4mg)
Calcium: 7% (72.8mg)
Iron: 13% (2.3mg)
Magnesium: 27% (109mg)
Phosphorus: 23% (226mg)
Potassium: 12% (409mg)
Zinc: 12% (1.7mg)
Copper: 21% (.4mg)
Manganese: 69% (1.4mg)
Selenium: 11% (8mcg)

1. Preheat the oven to 325° F.

2. In a bowl, mix the water and flaxseeds and let them soak for an hour. Place the mixture in a medium-sized pot and bring it to a boil, uncovered, on the stove. Reduce the heat and simmer for 20 minutes. Strain the flaxseeds using a sieve and set the liquid mixture aside.

3. In a grinder, grind the oats and cashews into a smooth flour. Transfer the flour to a small mixing bowl and stir in the cinnamon, lemon zest, and carob powder. Combine with 1/3 apple juice.

4. Press the crust mixture firmly and evenly into an oiled pie tin. Set aside.

5. In a separate bowl, blend the 1/2 cup flax liquid, remaining apple juice, rice milk, date puree, nut butter, lemon juice, and vanilla using a handheld blender. Using a whisk, beat the mixture until frothy.

6. Pour the pie filling into the pie crust and top with pecans. Bake in the preheated oven for about 35 minutes or until the top of the pie is thoroughly cooked, making sure to not burn the crust. Let the pie cool completely before serving. Serve!

Makes 8 servings or one pie

Vanilla Muffins

This basic recipe for vanilla muffins is kept healthy with whole wheat pastry flour and apple juice. In addition to being eaten as desserts, these muffins can be eaten as snacks or for breakfast.

- **2 cups whole wheat pastry flour**

  ⭐ *Spelt option: Use 2 1/4 cups spelt flour and an extra 1/4 tsp baking powder and 1/4 tsp baking soda*

- **1 tsp baking powder**

- **1 tsp baking soda**

- **1/2 tsp salt**

- **1 1/2 cup apple juice concentrate**

- **1/2 cup rice milk or other milk**

- **2 tsp vanilla extract**

- **1/4 cup cashew butter**

1. Preheat the oven to 375° F.

2. In a medium-sized mixing bowl, mix the flour, baking powder, baking soda, and salt.

3. In a smaller bowl, combine the apple juice, rice milk, vanilla, and nut butter using a handheld blender.

4. Mix the apple juice mixture into the dry ingredients and "fluff" the batter, being careful not to overmix it.

5. Line a normal-sized muffin tin with 10 baking cups and spoon equal amounts of the batter into each of the baking cups.

6. Bake the muffins for about 15 minutes in the preheated oven. Remove them from the tin and let them cool. Serve!

Makes 10 muffins

* You can also make a cake using this recipe. At step 5, pour the batter into an oiled 8 x 8 pan instead of a muffin tin and bake for an extra 15 minutes or until a toothpick comes out clean.

Nutritional Info
(Per 1/10 of recipe, 66g):

Calories: 177
Fat: 4g (6%)
Sodium: 298mg (2%)
Carbohydrates: 33g (11%)
Fiber: 3g
Sugars: 13g
Protein: 5g
Omega 3: 26.5mg
Riboflavin: 5% (.1mg)
Niacin: 8% (1.7mg)
B6: 7% (.1mg)
Folate: 4% (15.2mcg)
B5: 4% (.4mcg)
Calcium: 4% (44.2mg)
Iron: 9% (1.6mg)
Magnesium: 14% (55.6mg)
Phosphorus: 13% (131mg)
Potassium: 8% (284mg)
Zinc: 7% (1.1mg)
Copper: 12% (.2mg)
Manganese: 52% (1mg)
Selenium: 25% (17.8mcg)

Banana Plum Salad (p. 113)

Coconut Pear Ice Cream (p. 115)

Fruit for Dessert

Fruit makes some of the best desserts. Sweet, healthy, and tasty; it pleases easily. The following recipes require very little preparation and can be made easily, which makes them good for everyday desserts.

AvoCarob Pudding

Avocado and strawberries give this pudding a lovely rich and fruity flavor and keep it nutritious. But make sure no one gives Fido a taste; avocado is poisonous for dogs and cats.

- **1 large avocado, chopped**
- **1/2 cup chopped strawberries**
- **2 tbsp date puree**
- **1/4 cup apple juice concentrate**
- **1/4 cup carob or cocoa powder**

1. In a mixing bowl, blend the avocado, strawberries, dates, juice, and carob until smooth using a handheld blender.

2. Transfer the mixture to individual serving bowls and chill in the refrigerator. Serve!

Makes 4 servings

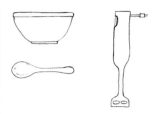

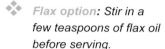

❖ *Flax option: Stir in a few teaspoons of flax oil before serving.*

Nutritional Info
(per 1/4 serving 96g):

Calories: 140
Fat: 8g (12%)
Sodium: 10mg (0%)
Carbohydrates: 22g (7%)
Fiber: 8g
Sugars: 13g
Protein: 2g
Omega 3: 70.7mg
VA: 2% (77.3IU)
VC: 28% (16.5mg)
VE: 6% (1.2mg)
VK: 14% (11.1mcg)
Thiamin: 3% (.0mg)
Riboflavin: 7% (.1mg)
Niacin: 6% (1.2mg)
B6: 10% (.2mg)
Folate: 12% (48.7mcg)
B5: 8% (.8mg)
Calcium: 4% (44.6mg)
Iron: 4% (.8mg)
Magnesium: 6% (25.8mg)
Phosphorus: 4% (43.5mg)
Potassium: 12% (433mg)
Zinc: 3% (.5mg)
Copper: 9% (.2mg)
Manganese: 12% (.2mg)

Banana Plum Salad

This fruit salad is best for the summer months when plums are in season.

- **2 tbsp pecans**
- **1/2 tsp cinnamon**
- **4 plums, chopped**
- **2 bananas, sliced**
- **2 tbsp apple juice concentrate**
- **2 tbsp orange juice concentrate**
- **1/2 tsp lemon zest**
- **1 tbsp shredded coconut (unsweetened or sweetened)**

1. In a small bowl, mix the pecans with the cinnamon until the pecans are evenly coated with cinnamon. Toast the pecans on a small baking tray in a toaster oven at 350° F for about 5 minutes, being careful to not burn them. Meanwhile, follow the steps below.

2. In a medium-sized mixing bowl, mix the plums, bananas, and juices. Make sure the banana is well-coated with juice to prevent it from browning.

3. Place the fruit in a serving bowl and sprinkle the pecans, coconut, and lemon zest on top. Serve!

Makes 4 servings

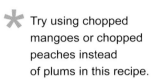

 Try using chopped mangoes or chopped peaches instead of plums in this recipe.

❖ *Flax option: Stir in 2-3 tsp of flax oil at step 2 or sprinkle with flax meal before serving.*

Nutritional Info
(per 1/4th recipe, 135g)

Calories: 174
Fat: 8g (12%)
Sodium: 4mg (0%)
Carbohydrates: 27g (9%)
Fiber: 4g
Sugars: 19g
Protein: 2g
Omega 3: 87.9mg
VA: 5% (247IU)
VC: 37% (22.4mg)
VE: 2% (.4mg)
VK: 5% (3.9mcg)
Thiamin: 7% (.1mg)
Riboflavin: 5% (.1mg)
Niacin: 4% (.8mg)
B6: 14% (.3mg)
Folate: 7% (30mcg)
B5: 4% (.4mg)
Calcium: 2% (19.1mg)
Iron: 4% (.7mg)
Magnesium: 9% (35.5mg)
Phosphorous: 5% (54.7mg)
Potassium: 12% (429mg)
Zinc: 4% (.6mg)
Copper: 10% (.2mg)
Manganese: 34% (.7mg)
Selenium: 2% (1.6mcg)

Cinnamon Apple Salad

Shredded apples give this salad a nice, soft texture close to that of apple sauce, but with half the work. Here, they are tossed with dates, cinnamon, and pecans to make a quick dessert that's healthy to boot.

- **4 apples, shredded**

- **1/3 cup lemon or lime juice**

- **1/4 cup pecans**

- **1 tsp cinnamon**

- **12 soft dates, chopped into small pieces**

- **Cinnamon to taste**

1. In a small mixing bowl, toss the apple with the lemon juice. Cover the bowl to minimize exposure to air and set aside.

2. In a separate mixing bowl, mix the pecans with the cinnamon until they are evenly coated with cinnamon. Toast the pecans on a small baking tray in a toaster oven at 350º F for about 5 minutes, being careful to not burn them.

3. Add the toasted pecans and chopped dates to the apple mixture and toss. Sprinkle with cinnamon. Serve!

Makes 1 serving

 Granny Smith apples (green apple) work nicely here. Their sour taste seems to add the right contrast to the dates and cinnamon. A nice sweet, red apple could work well here too. Make sure to pick a firm, unblemished apple

❖ *Flax option: Stir in 1 tsp of flax oil at step 3 or sprinkle with flax meal before serving.*

Nutritional Info
(per 1/4 recipe, 239g):

Calories: 260
Fat: 11g (16%)
Sodium: 3mg (0%)
Carbohydrates: 46g (15%)
Fiber: 8g, Sugars: 33g
Protein: 2g
Omega 3: 156mg
VA: 2% (116IU)
VC: 31% (18.3mg)
VE: 3% (.6mg)
VK: 7% (5.5mcg)
Thiamin: 9% (.1mg)
Riboflavin: 5% (.1mg)
Niacin: 3% (.6mg)
B6: 8% (.2mg)
Folate: 4% (15.4mcg)
B5: 4% (.4mg)
Calcium: 4% (43mg)
Iron: 5% (.9mg)
Magnesium: 9% (37.2mg)
Phosphorus: 7% (74.2mg)
Potassium: 12% (422mg)
Copper: 14% (.3mg)
Manganese: 49% (1mg)
Selenium: 2% (1.2mg)

Coconut Pear Ice Cream

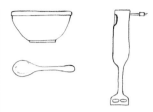

This ice cream makes a luscious, creamy summertime treat. Serve it with fresh summertime fruit to make a succulent dessert.

- **1/2 cup coconut milk**

- **1 1/2 cup chopped canned pears (drained of juice)**

1. In a mixing bowl, use a handheld blender to blend the coconut milk and canned pears until smooth. Spoon into a plastic freezer bag.

2. Place the plastic bag in the freezer. Every 15 minutes or so, take the bag out and agitate the coconut mixture so no lumps form in the mixture and everything is evenly frozen. Do this for about an hour and a half or until the ice cream has reached the desired consistency. Serve!

Makes 1 serving

* You can make popsicles with this recipe by pouring the ice cream mixture into a popsicle mold and letting it freeze until solid.

* For a soft-serve ice cream consistency, this mixture may take less than an hour to reach the right consistency. For a firmer consistency, the mixture may take up to the full amount of time to reach the correct consistency.

Nutritional Info
(per 1/4 recipe, 121g):

Calories: 102
Fat: 6g (9%)
Sodium: 7mg (0%)
Carbohydrates: 13g (4%)
Fiber: 1g
Sugars: 9g
Protein: 1g
Omega 3: 0mg
VC: 3% (1.8mg)
Niacin: 2% (.4mg)
Iron: 7% (1.2mg)
Magnesium: 5% (19.5mg)
Phosphorous: 4% (38.3mg)
Potassium: 4% (151mg)
Zinc: 2% (.2mg)
Copper: 6% (.1mg)
Manganese: 12% (.2mg)

Pomegranate Clementine Salad

Sweet and tangy, this fruit salad is wonderfully refreshing. A pomegranates is a round, purple/red fruit about the size of a grapefruit that contains sweet, juicy seeds that appear gem-like to the eye.

- **Seeds of one pomegranate**

- **5 clementines, peeled and sectioned**

- **Juice of 2 oranges**

- **1/2 tsp cinnamon**

1. In a mixing bowl, mix the pomegranate seeds, clementines, orange juice, and cinnamon.

2. Cover the bowl with plastic wrap and refrigerate the salad for at least 30 minutes. Serve!

Makes 6 servings

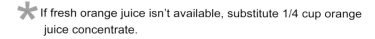 If fresh orange juice isn't available, substitute 1/4 cup orange juice concentrate.

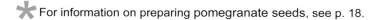 For information on preparing pomegranate seeds, see p. 18.

Nutritional Info
(per 1/6 recipe, 169g):

Calories: 60
Fat: 0g
Sodium: 2mg (0%)
Carbohydrates: 15g (5%)
Fiber: 1g
Sugars: 12g
Protein: 1g
Omega 3: 3.2mg
VA: 2% (85.7IU)
VC: 77% (46mg)
VK: 2% (1.3mcg)
Thiamin: 6% (.1mg)
Riboflavin: 2% (.0mg)
Niacin: 3% (.6mg)
B6: 4% (.1mg)
Folate: 6% (25mcg)
B5: 3% (.3mg)
Calcium: 2% (24.5mg)
Magnesium: 3% (10.2mg)
Phosphorus: 2% (20mg)
Potassium: 7% (234mg)
Copper: 3% (.1mg)
Manganese: 3% (.1mg)

Sesame Sugarplum Squares

Sugarplums, which are a mixture of dried fruits and nuts, are traditionally formed into balls and then rolled in sugar. This twist on the old favorite makes squares instead of balls and is topped with sesame seeds instead of sugar.

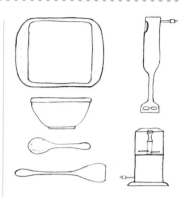

- **1/2 cup dried cranberries**
- **1/2 cup raisins**
- **1/2 cup dates**
- **1/2 cup dried apricots**
- **1 cup raw almonds**
- **1/2 cup walnuts**
- **2 tbsp orange juice concentrate**
- **3 tbsp sesame seeds for topping**

1. Put the cranberries, raisins, dates, and apricots in a small mixing bowl and cover them with water. Soak for about 30 minutes or until the fruit is soft. Drain.

2. In a grinder, grind the almonds and walnuts into a paste (You may need to do this in two separate batches.). Transfer to a mixing bowl and set aside.

3. Using a food processor or a handheld blender, puree the dried fruit into a chunky puree.

4. Mix the dried fruit puree into the nut mixture. Add the orange juice concentrate and mix thoroughly.

5. Firmly and evenly press the fruit and nut mixture into an 8 x 8 pan. Sprinkle with the sesame seeds.

6. Cover the pan with plastic wrap and refrigerate for one to two days or until the mixture hardens. Cut into 16 squares using a knife. Serve!

Makes 16 squares

 If you wish, you can slice these into bars instead of squares.

 Feel free to try different combinations of dried fruit and nuts rather than the ones suggested here.

Nutritional Info
(per 1/16 recipe, 34g):

Calories: 109
Fat: 5g (7%)
Carbohydrates: 17g (6%)
Fiber: 2g, Sugars: 13g
Protein: 2g
Omega 3: 335mg
VA: 2% (107IU)
VC: 4% (2.6mg)
VE: 7% (1.4mg)
Thiamin: 2% (.0mg)
Riboflavin: 4% (.1mg)
Niacin: 2% (.4mg)
B6: 3% (.1mg)
Folate: 2% (9.9mcg)
Calcium: 2% (22.5mg)
Iron: 3% (.5mg)
Magnesium: 6% (23.2mg)
Phosphorus: 5% (45.8mg)
Potassium: 5% (163mg)
Zinc: 2% (.3mg)
Manganese: 14% (.3mg)

Breakfast

Perfect Pancakes (p. 129)

Quinoa Granola (p. 128)

Good Morning!

Nutritionists tell us that breakfast is the most important meal of the day. Start the day off right with the healthy recipes in this chapter, all of which are whole grain and free of added sugar.

A+ Rice Pudding

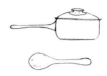

This rice pudding is made with apricots and almonds, thus the moniker "A+" Rice Pudding. Use leftover rice rather than freshly cooked rice for convenience.

- **1 cup chopped, dried apricots**
- **1/2 cup almonds**
- **3 cups almond milk**
- **3 cups cooked brown rice**
- **1/3 cup apple juice concentrate**
- **1 tsp cinnamon**

1. In a medium-sized pot, mix the apricots, almonds, almond milk, rice, juice, and cinnamon.

2. Bring the mixture to a boil, uncovered. Then reduce the heat and simmer the pudding for about 25 minutes. Serve!

Makes 6 servings

 To make almond milk, combine 3 cups water with 3/4 cup almonds, ground into flour.

Nutritional Info
(per 1/6 recipe, 286g):

Calories: 251,
Fat: 8g (13%)
Sodium: 15mg (1%)
Carbohydrates: 41g (14%)
Fiber: 5g
Sugars: 15g
Protein: 6g
Omega 3: 17.2mg
VA: 15% (533IU)
VE: 39% (4.5mg)
Thiamin: 8% (.1mg)
Riboflavin: 8% (.2mg)
B6: 10% (.2mg)
Folate: 2% (12.5mcg)
B5: 4% (.5mg)
Calcium: 14% (66.2mg)
Iron: 8% (1.5mg)
Magnesium: 20% (88.9mg)
Phosphorus: 16% (165mg)
Potassium: 10% (379mg)
Zinc: 7% (1.2mg)
Copper: 12% (.3mg)
Manganese: 61% (1.4mg)
Selenium: 15% (10.3mcg)

Amaranth Bran Muffins

These moist bran muffins are flavored with tiny amaranth, a flavorful grain used to make a well known liqueur called Amaretto. These muffins make filling breakfasts and snacks.

- **1 1/2 cup wheat bran**
- **2/3 cup water**
- **1 cup whole wheat pastry flour**
- **1/4 cup amaranth flour**
- **1/2 tsp salt**
- **1 tsp baking soda**
- **1 tsp baking powder**
- **1 tsp cinnamon**
- **1 1/2 cup apple juice concentrate**
- **1/3 cup peanut butter**

1. Preheat the oven to 375° F.

2. In a small pot, bring the water to a boil. Place the bran in a small mixing bowl and stir the water into it. Let the mixture rest for 5 to 10 minutes.

3. In a medium-sized mixing bowl, mix the flours, salt, baking soda, and cinnamon. Set aside.

4. In a separate mixing bowl, combine the juice and peanut butter with the help of a handheld blender.

5. Stir the apple juice mixture into the dry ingredients, being careful to not overmix. Add the bran mixture and "fluff" the batter.

6. Line a regular-sized muffin tin with baking cups. Spoon equal amounts of batter into 12 baking cups.

7. Bake the muffins in the preheated oven for about 25 minutes or until a toothpick comes out clean. Let cool. Serve!

Makes 12 muffins.

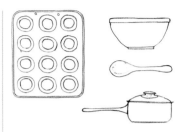

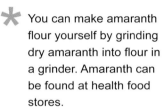

* You can make amaranth flour yourself by grinding dry amaranth into flour in a grinder. Amaranth can be found at health food stores.

❖ *Flax option: Stir in 1/4 cup flax meal at step 5.*

Nutritional Info
(per 1/12 recipe, 61g):

Calories: 134
Fat: 5g (7%)
Sodium: 187mg (8%)
Carbohydrates: 23g (8%)
Fiber: 4g, Sugars: 12g
Protein: 4g
Omega 3: 26.2mg
VE: 4% (.8mg)
Thiamin: 3% (.1mg)
Riboflavin: 4% (.1mg)
Niacin: 11% (2.2mg)
B6: 9% (.2mg)
Folate: 4% (14.2mcg)
B5: 4% (.4mg)
Calcium: 2% (22.8mg)
Iron: 9% (1.6mg)
Magnesium: 18% (74mg)
Phosphorus: 13% (130mg)
Potassium: 8% (281mg)
Zinc: 6% (.9mg)
Copper: 8% (.2mg)
Manganese: 57% (1.1mg)
Selenium: 9% (6.2mcg)

Apricot 'n Almond Spread

This sweet, comforting spread is great with toast.

- **1/2 cup soft, dried apricots**
- **2 tbsp almond butter**
- **2 1/2 tbsp apple juice concentrate**
- **1/2 tsp cinnamon**

1. In a mixing bowl, puree the apricots, nut butter, juice, and cinnamon until smooth using a handheld blender. Serve!

Makes 4 servings or 1/2 cup spread

 To make the apricots soft, soak them overnight in a small bowl filled with water.

Nutritional Info (per 1/4 recipe, 48g):

Calories: 92, Fat: 5g (7%)
Sodium: 4mg (0%), Carbohydrates: 12g (4%)
Fiber: 1g (5%), Sugars: 10g, Protein: 2g
Omega 3: 35.5mg, VA: 8% (398IU)
VE: 2% (.5mg), Riboflavin: 4% (.1mg)
Niacin: 3% (.5mg), B6: 2% (.0mg)
Folate: 2% (6.2mcg), Calcium: 3% (29.2mg)
Iron: 4% (.7mg), Magnesium: 7% (29.2mg)
Phosphorus: 7% (51.8mg)
Potassium: 5% (228mg), Zinc: 2% (.3mg)
Copper: 6% (.1mg), Manganese: 12% (.2mg)

Gingery Date Spread

This yummy fruit spread has a nice 'n spicy taste to it. It's just the thing to wake you up in the morning.

- **1 cup soft dates**
- **1 1/2 tsp ground ginger**
- **1 tbsp lemon juice**
- **1 tbsp almond butter**

1. In a mixing bowl, puree the dates, ginger, lemon juice and almond butter until smooth using a handheld blender. Serve!

Makes 4 servings or 1/2 cup spread

 Soak dates overnight in a small bowl filled with water to soften them and make them easier to puree.

Nutritional Info (per 2 tbsp, 58g):

Calories: 172, Fat: 3g (5%)
Sodium: 2mg (0%), Carbs: 38g (13%)
Fiber: 4g, Sugars: 30g, Protein: 2g
VC: 4% (2.5mg), VK: 2% (1.3mcg)
Thiamin: 2% (.0mg), Riboflavin: 4% (.1mg)
Niacin: 4% (.8mg), B6: 5% (.1mg)
Folate: 3% (13.4mcg), B5: 3% (.3mg)
Calcium: 3% (34mg), Iron: 4% (.8mg)
Magnesium: 10% (38.2mg)
Phosphorus: 6% (58.4mg)
Potassium: 11% (58.4mg)
Zinc: 2% (.3mg), Copper: 8% (.2mg)
Manganese: 24% (.5mg)
Selenium: 3% (1.8mcg)

Breakfast Bread Pudding

I love bread pudding! Not only is it an easy way to finish off a loaf of stale bread, it tastes wonderful and is family friendly. Serve it in bowls with coconut milk drizzled on top. Mmm…

- **1 apple, chopped**

- **1/4 cup apple juice concentrate**

- **3 bananas**

- **1 cup rice milk or other milk**

- **1 tsp pumpkin pie spice**

- **1 tsp vanilla extract**

- **1/2 tsp almond extract**

- **6 cups 1 inch stale whole grain bread cubes**

  Gluten-free option: Use gluten-free whole grain bread.

- **1/4 cup dried cranberries**

- **1/4 cup slivered almonds**

1. Preheat the oven to 350° F.

2. In a small pot, mix the apple juice and chopped apple. Bring the mixture to a boil, reduce heat, and simmer until the apple is soft. Set aside.

3. In a mixing bowl, blend the bananas, rice milk, and seasonings until smooth using a handheld blender. Stir in the cubed bread, apple mixture, and cranberries.

4. Spoon mixture into an oiled 8 x 8 baking pan. Cover the pan with plastic wrap and refrigerate overnight, or for at least 1 hour.

5. Remove the plastic wrap and sprinkle the almonds on top of the pudding. Bake in the preheated oven for about 40 minutes or until the pudding has set. Serve!

Makes 16 servings

❖ *Flax option: Stir in 2 tbsp flax meal at step 3.*

Nutritional Info
(per 1/16 recipe, 140g):

Calories: 293
Fat: 6g (9%)
Sodium: 297mg (12%)
Carbohydrates: 56g (19%)
Fiber: 6g
Sugars: 11g
Protein: 8g
VC: 4% (2.6mg)
VE: 6% (1.2mg)
VK: 11% (8.4mcg)
Thiamin: 18% (.3mg)
Riboflavin: 14% (.2mg)
Niacin: 18% (3.6mg)
B6: 13% (.3mg)
Folate: 15% (60.3mcg)
B5: 5% (.5mg)
Calcium: 4% (36.9mg)
Iron: 16% (2.8mg)
Magnesium: 20% (80mg)
Potassium: 11% (385mg)
Zinc: 9% (1.4mg)
Copper: 13% (.3mg)
Manganese: 86% (1.7mg)
Selenium: 47% (32.7mg)

Cranberry Tahini Oatmeal

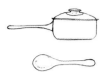

This delicious oatmeal makes a hearty, wintertime breakfast.

- **1 cup water**
- **1/2 cup old fashioned oats**
- **Pinch of salt**
- **1/4 cup cranberry sauce**
- **2 tbsp tahini**

1. In a small pot, mix the water, salt, and half of the oats. Bring to a boil. Stir in the remaining oats and let cook for about five minutes. Cover and set aside for 3 minutes.

2. Transfer the cooked oatmeal to an individual serving bowl. Spoon the cranberry sauce on top and drizzle on the tahini. Serve!

Makes 1 serving

 To make homemade cranberry sauce, combine 2 parts fresh cranberries to 1 part orange juice concentrate (chopped Clementine pieces can be added if desired) and 1 part date puree in a medium-size pot. Bring the mixture to a boil and let it simmer until all the berries "pop". Simmer to the desired consistency. This can be stored up to a week in the refrigerator

 Flax option: Stir 1 tbsp of flax meal into oatmeal at step 2 before adding cranberry sauce.

Nutritional info
(per whole recipe, 333g):

Calories: 393,
Fat: 19g (29%)
Sodium: 47mg (2%)
Carbohydrates: 50g (17%)
Fiber: 8g, Sugars: 14g
Protein: 11g
Omega 3: 168mg
VA: 2% (95.8mg)
VC: 44% (26.2mg)
VE: 3% (.5mg)
VK: 2% (1.8mcg)
Thiamin: 41% (.6mg)
Riboflavin: 13% (.2mg)
Niacin: 12% (2.3mg)
B6: 7% (.1mg)
Folate: 18% (71.7mg)
B5: 9% (.9mg)
Calcium: 17% (166mg)
Iron: 26% (4.6mg)
Magnesium: 24% (97.4mg)
Phosphorus: 40% (403mg)
Potassium: 13% (461mg)
Zinc: 20% (3mg)
Copper: 36% (.7mg)
Manganese: 99% (2mg)
Selenium: 18% (12.6mg)

Fruit'n Nut Bars

These sweet, nutty bars are held together by orange juice that has been reduced into syrup. The orange syrup can be used as a topping for pancakes and can replace maple syrup or light corn syrup in some recipes.

- **1 cup orange juice concentrate**
- **2 tsp lemon juice**
- **1/2 tsp cinnamon**
- **1/4 cup sesame seeds**
- **1/2 cup almonds**

- **1/2 cup walnuts**
- **1/2 cup shelled pistachios**
- **1/2 cup cashews**
- **3/4 cup raisins**

1. Preheat the oven to 350° F.

2. In a large mixing bowl, mix the sesame seeds, almonds, walnuts, cashews, pistachios, and raisins.

3. In a small pot, combine the orange juice, lemon juice, and cinnamon and bring to a boil. Let the mixture boil until it's reduced into syrup. Be very careful to watch the mixture when it boils as it can burn easily. Use a fork to test the thickness of the liquid by dipping the tip of the fork into the liquid and then setting it aside. If the liquid dries thickly on the fork, it is the right consistency.

4. Mix the orange syrup into the nut mixture, making sure all the nuts and the raisins are evenly coated. Work quickly as the syrup mixture dries out after a few minutes.

5. Firmly and evenly press the fruit and nut mixture into an oiled 8 x 8 pan. Bake for 15 minutes in the preheated oven.
Remove from oven and let cool for about 30 minutes or until completely cool. Cut into 8 bars. Serve!

Makes 8 bars

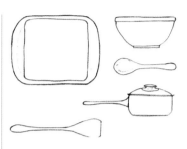

* It's preferable to use raw and unsalted nuts and seeds for this recipe as the nuts will be toasted after being formed into bars.

Nutritional Info
(per 1/8 recipe, 94g):

Calories: 348,
Fat: 21g (32%)
Sodium: 5mg (0%)
Carbohydrates: 37g (12%)
Fiber: 4g
Sugars: 24g
Protein: 9g
Omega 3: 715mg
VA: 4% (180IU)
VC: 84% (50.1mg)
VE: 15% (3mg)
VK: 7% (5.7mg)
Thiamin: 21% (.3mg)
Riboflavin: 10% (.2mg)
Niacin: 6% (1.2mg)
B6: 18% (.4mg)
Folate: 20% (79.7mcg)
B5: 5% (.5mg)
Calcium: 11% (109mg)
Iron: 16% (2.9mg)
Magnesium: 30% (115mg)
Phosphorus: 25% (263mg)
Potassium: 18% (509mg)
Zinc: 13% (1.9mg)
Copper: 45% (.5mg)
Manganese: 49% (1.5mg)
Selenium: 6% (11.6mcg)

Quinoa Granola

Quinoa adds crunch to this yummy granola. Serve this granola with rice or almond milk for a simple breakfast.

- **2 cups rolled oats**
- **2 cups rinsed, dry quinoa (p. 19)**
- **1 cup apple juice concentrate**
- **1 1/2 tbsp sesame oil**
- **2 bananas, pureed until smooth**
- **1 tsp vanilla extract**
- **1 tsp pumpkin pie spice**
- **1/3 cup shredded coconut (sweetened or unsweetened)**
- **1/3 cup unsalted, raw sunflower seeds**
- **2/3 cup raisins**

1. Preheat the oven to 350° F.

2. In a medium-sized mixing bowl, mix the oats and quinoa. Transfer the grain mixture to a baking tray and spread into one even layer. Toast the mixture in the oven for ten minutes, stirring the mixture every three minutes. Meanwhile, follow steps three and four.

3. In a small pot, bring the apple juice concentrate to a boil. Let the juice boil until it is reduced into syrup. Be very careful to constantly watch the mixture when it boils as it burns easily. Use a fork to test the thickness of the liquid by dipping the tip of the fork into the liquid and then setting it aside. If the liquid dries thickly on the fork, it is the right consistency.

4. Transfer the apple juice concentrate to a large bowl and stir in the sesame oil, bananas, vanilla, and pumpkin pie spice. Add the toasted oats, coconut, and sunflower seeds, making sure everything is well-coated with apple juice mixture.

5. Transfer the mixture to a baking tray and bake for 10 minutes in the preheated oven or until golden brown. Remove from the oven and cool. Store in an airtight container in the fridge. Serve!

Makes 12 servings

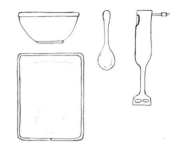

* If desired, additional oats can be substituted for quinoa.

* Dried fruit and nuts of choice can be used instead of sunflower seeds and raisins.

❖ *Flax option: Stir 1 tbsp flax meal into a bowl of granola before eating.*

Nutritional Info
(per 1/12 recipe, 104g):

Calories: 332, Fat: 13g (19%)
Sodium: 11mg (0%)
Carbohydrates: 49g (16%)
Fiber: 6g, Sugars: 15g
Protein: 8g, Omega 3: 120mg
VC: 4% (2.5mg)
VE: 16% (3.2mg)
Thiamin: 19% (.3mg)
Riboflavin: 10% (.2mg)
Niacin: 7% (1.4mg)
B6: 19% (.4mg)
Folate: 19% (77.6mcg)
B5: 6% (.6mg)
Calcium: 4% (37.3mg)
Iron: 16% (2.9mg)
Magnesium: 29% (115mg)
Phosphorus: 26% (263mg)
Potassium: 15% (509mg)
Zinc: 13% (1.9mg)
Copper: 23% (.5mg)
Manganese: 77% (1.5mg)
Selenium: 17% (11.6mcg)

Perfect Pancakes

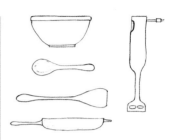

These light, fluffy pancakes make a delicious breakfast for special occasions and for everyday.

- **2 cups whole wheat pastry flour**

  Spelt option: Use 2 1/4 cups spelt flour in place of wheat flour

- **1 tsp baking soda**
- **1 tsp baking powder**
- **1/2 tsp salt**
- **1 tsp vanilla extract**
- **1 medium banana**
- **1/2 cup apple juice concentrate**
- **1 1/4 cup rice milk or other milk**
- **2 tbsp cashew butter**
- **1/2 cup fresh fruit (berries, pears, peaches, bananas, etc.)**
- **1/2 tbsp canola oil**

1. In a medium-sized mixing bowl, mix the flour, baking soda, baking powder, and salt.

2. In a smaller mixing bowl, blend the banana, juice, rice milk, and nut butter until smooth using a handheld blender.

3. Mix the rice milk mixture into the dry ingredients. Stir in the fruit.

4. Heat the canola oil in a skillet until hot. To make sure the skillet is hot enough, pour a few drops of water onto the skillet. The water should "split".

5. Pour the desired amount of batter (I recommend using a ladle full of batter for a 4 inch pancake.) onto the skillet. Cook the pancake until air bubbles appear on the top side of the pancake and the edges of the pancake are no longer raw and gooey. Flip the pancake and cook it for a few more minutes. Repeat this step with the rest of the batter, adding more oil to the skillet if necessary. Serve!

Makes 4 servings, with 2 to 3 four inches pancakes per person

 Make cornmeal pancakes by using equal parts oat flour and cornmeal rather than wheat flour, adding more of the mixture if the batter is too thin. Omit the vanilla extract and handle them carefully while cooking.

 Flax option: Stir in 2 tbsp flax meal at step 3.

Nutritional Info
(per 1/4 recipe, 181g):

Calories: 363
Fat: 4g (7%)
Sodium: 501mg (21%)
Carbohydrates: 77g (26%)
Fiber: 9g, Sugars: 11g
Protein: 12g
Omega 3: 132mg
VC: 6% (3.5mg)
VK: 4% (3.3mcg)
Thiamin: 2% (0mg)
Riboflavin: 2% (.0mg)
B6: 6% (.1mg)
Folate: 2% (8.5mcg)
B5: 2% (.2mg)
Calcium: 6% (55.9mg)
Iron: 20% (3.5mg)
Magnesium: 6% (23.3mg)
Phosphorus: 5% (51.3mg)
Potassium: 6% (194mg)
Zinc: 2% (.4mg)
Copper: 7% (.1mg)
Manganese: 7% (.2mg)

Beverages

Strawberry Watermelon Smoothie (p.139)

Hot Almond Banana Drink (p. 137)

Cheers!

... for healthy beverages everyone can enjoy. Now that's a reason to be cheerful! Here you'll find healthy smoothies made with fruits and vegetables, hot drinks for wintertime and much more.

Bugs Bunny Smoothie

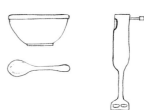

Bugs Bunny, the famous Looney Tunes character, would love this nutritious smoothie that's chockfull of carrots. One thing is for sure, he won't be saying "What's up, doc?" any time soon after drinking this smoothie.

- **1/2 medium banana**
- **1/2 cup packed finely shredded carrots**
- **3 tbsp rice milk or other milk**
- **1/2 tbsp wheat germ (optional)**
- **2 tsp lemon juice**
- **Finely chopped clementines and poppy seeds for topping (optional)**
- **Shredded coconut and raisins for topping (optional)**

1. In a mixing bowl, puree the carrots and banana until smooth using a handheld blender. Be careful that you don't overwork your handheld blender while doing this.

2. Add the rice milk, wheat germ, and lemon juice to the carrot mixture and blend until smooth.

3. Pour the smoothie into a large serving glass and top with clementines and poppy seeds or coconut and raisins. Serve!

Makes 1 serving

 This recipe can be easily doubled, tripled, and quadrupled to serve more people.

❖ *Flax option: Stir in a few teaspoons of flax oil before serving. You can also replace the wheat germ with flax meal.*

Nutritional Info
(per whole recipe, 175g):

Calories: 143,
Fat: 4g (5%)
Sodium: 55mg (0%)
Carbohydrates: 28g (9%)
Fiber: 4g, Sugars: 10g
Protein: 3g
Omega 3: 1219mg
VA: 185% (9228IU)
VC: 22% (13.5mg)
VE: 4% (.8mg)
VK: 9% (7.6mg)
Thiamin: 13% (.2mg)
Riboflavin: 7% (.1mg)
Niacin: 7% (1.4mg)
B6: 19% (.4mg)
Folate: 11% (43.3mcg)
B5: 5% (.5mg)
Calcium: 3% (28.1mg)
Iron: 4% (.8mg)
Magnesium: 10% (39.9mg)
Phosphorus: 9% (91.8mg)
Potassium: 13% (463mg)
Zinc: 7% (1.1mg)
Copper: 6% (.1mg)
Manganese: 58% (1.2mg)
Selenium: 9% (6.2mcg)

Fruity Lemonade

This combination of sweet, velvety, fruit juice with sour lemon juice makes for a tangy, refreshing drink.

- **3/4 cup fruit juice of choice (pineapple, peach, orange, or mango)**

- **2 tbsp lemon juice**

- **1/4 cup frozen grapes (preferably red grapes- they add color)**

1. In a serving glass, combine the juices. Stir in the frozen grapes. Serve!

Makes 1 serving

 This recipe can be easily doubled, tripled, and quadrupled to serve more people.

Nutritional info
(per whole recipe, 253g):

Calories: 117
Fat: 0g (0%)
Sodium: 3mg
Carbohydrates: 29g (10%)
Fiber: 1g
Sugars: 22g
Protein: 2g
Omega 3: 24.6mg
VA: 8% (403IU)
VC: 183% (110mg)
VK: 7% (5.7mcg)
Thiamin: 13% (.2mg)
Riboflavin: 5% (.1mg)
Niacin: 4% (.8mg)
B6: 6% (.1mg)
Folate: 15% (60.2mcg)
B5: 4% (.4mg)
Calcium: 3% (26.2mg)
Iron: 3% (.5mg)
Magnesium: 6% (24.8mg)
Phosphorus: 4% (40.9mg)
Potassium: 14% (479mg)
Copper: 7% (.1mg)
Manganese: 3% (.1mg)

Nutritional info is
calculated with orange
juice.

Green Mango Lassi

This fruity smoothie is a great way to eat your greens.

- **1/2 cup chopped ripe mango**
- **1/2 cup packed spinach, finely chopped**
- **1/3 cup rice milk or other milk**
- **1/2 tbsp apple juice concentrate**
- **Pinch of nutmeg**
- **1 tsp lemon juice (optional)**

1. In a medium-sized mixing bowl, puree the mango until smooth using a handheld blender.

2. Add the spinach and continue to blend, being careful not to overwork your handheld blender. Gradually add the rice milk, juice, nutmeg, and lemon juice (Tip: Make sure the spinach is completely blended into a puree, this smoothie's success is measured by its creaminess.).

3. Stir in the nutmeg. Pour smoothie into a serving glass and serve with a straw. Serve!

Makes 1 serving

 While this recipe only serves one, it can be easily doubled, tripled, and quadrupled to serve as many people as you like.

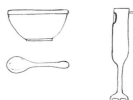

 Mango can be replaced by a medium banana.

Nutritional Info
(per whole recipe, 209g):

Calories: 116
Fat: 1g
Sodium: 57mg (2%)
Carbohydrates: 27g (9%)
Fiber: 2g
Sugars: 15g
Protein: 2g
VA: 69% (3495IU)
VC: 57% (32.5mg)
VE: 8% (1.5mg)
VK: 185% (148mcg)
Thiamin: 5% (.1mg)
Riboflavin: 6% (.1mg)
Niacin: 4% (.7mg)
B6: 9% (.2mg)
Folate: 18% (70.6mcg)
B5: 2% (.2mg)
Calcium: 5% (46.7mg)
Iron: 6% (1mg)
Magnesium: 8% (32.7mg)
Phosphorus: 3% (25.9mg)
Potassium: 10% (335mg)
Copper: 7% (.1mg)
Manganese: 15% (.3mg)

Hot Almond Banana Drink

This is a rich, substantial, hot drink perfect for cold winter days.

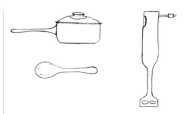

- **1 cup rice milk or other milk**

- **1 tsp almond butter**

- **Pinch nutmeg**

- **1/2 tsp cinnamon**

- **1 banana**

1. Combine the rice milk, almond butter, nutmeg, and cinnamon in a small pot. Heat to desired temperature.

2. Meanwhile, puree the banana until smooth using a handheld blender.

3. When the rice milk mixture is ready, remove it from heat and stir in the banana puree. Serve!

Makes 1 serving

 This recipe can be easily doubled, tripled, and quadrupled to serve more people.

 Make fruity popsicles: Pour fruity lemonade into a popsicle mold and freeze.

Nutritional Info
(per whole recipe, 348g):

Calories: 250
Fat: 5g
Sodium: 82mg (3%)
Carbohydrates: 52g (17%)
Fiber: 4g, Sugars: 14g
Protein: 3g
Omega 3: 52.3mg
VA: 2% (79.2IU)
VC: 19% (11.5mg)
Thiamin: 3% (.0mg)
Riboflavin: 7% (.1mg)
Niacin: 5% (.9mg)
B6: 22% (.4mg)
Folate: 7% (26.8mcg)
B5: 4% (.4mg)
Calcium: 5% (50.1mg)
Iron: 4% (.8mg)
Magnesium: 12% (47.2mg)
Phosphorus: 5% (51.9mg)
Potassium: 13% (464mg)
Zinc: 2% (.3mg)
Copper: 7% (.1mg)
Manganese: 32% (.6mg)
Selenium: 2% (1.2mcg)

Hot Carob Drink

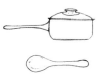

This drink is similar to hot chocolate. Serve it with fresh fruit instead of marshmallows.

- **1 cup rice milk or other milk**
- **1 1/2 tbsp carob or cocoa powder**
- **1 tbsp apple juice concentrate**
- **1/2 tsp vanilla extract**
- **1/4 tsp almond extract**

1. Combine the rice milk, carob, juice, and extracts in a medium-sized pot.

2. Heat until the desired temperature is reached, stirring occasionally. Serve!

Makes 4 servings

 This recipe can be easily doubled, tripled, and quadrupled to serve more people.

Nutritional Info
(per whole recipe, 269g):

Calories: 178
Fat: 2g (3%)
Sodium: 94mg (4%)
Carbohydrates: 42g (14%)
Fiber: 5g, Sugars: 12g
Protein: 2g
Omega 3: 3.2mg
VC: 3% (6.1mg)
VE: 2% (.3mg)
Thiamin: 2% (.0mg)
Riboflavin: 15% (.3mg)
Niacin: 5% (1mg)
B6: 12% (.2mg)
Folate: 4% (14.5mcg)
Calcium: 26% (259mg)
Iron: 15% (2.7mg)
Magnesium: 9% (36.8mg)
Potassium: 19% (664mg)
Copper: 16% (.3mg)
Manganese: 20% (.4mg)
Selenium: 4% (2.8mg)

Strawberry Watermelon Smoothie

This juicy smoothie is a light, refreshing drink that's perfect for summer.

- **1 cup cubed watermelon**

- **1/2 cup chopped strawberries**

- **1/4 cup frozen grapes**

- **Lime juice to taste**

1. In a medium-sized mixing bowl, blend the watermelon and strawberries until smooth using a handheld blender.

2. Pour into a serving glass and mix in the grapes and lime juice. Serve!

Makes 1 serving

* This recipe can be easily doubled, tripled, and quadrupled to serve more people.

* You can freeze the watermelon beforehand and blend it using a food processor instead of a handheld blender to make a slush-like drink.

* Make a fruity popsicle: Pour smoothie into a popsicle mold and freeze.

Nutritional Info
(per whole recipe, 267g)

Calories: 97
Fat: 1g (1%)
Sodium: 3mg (0%)
Carbohydrates: 24g (8%)
Fiber: 2g, Sugars: 19g
Protein: 2g
Omega 3: 53.6mg
VA: 18% (910IU)
VC: 102% (61.2mg)
VE: 2% (.4mg)
VK: 9% (7.3mcg)
Thiamin: 6% (.1mg)
Riboflavin: 4% (.1mg)
Niacin: 3% (.6mg)
B6: 7% (.1mg)
Folate: 6% (23.6mcg)
B5: 5% (.5mg)
Calcium: 3% (26.7mg)
Iron: 5% (.8mg)
Magnesium: 7% (27.9mg)
Phosphorus: 4% (42.7mg)
Potassium: 10% (361mg)
Zinc: 2% (.3mg)
Copper: 7% (.1mg)
Manganese: 19% (.4mg)

Ingredient Index

This index can be used to find recipes that use ingredients that you have on hand. You may want to see the Frequently Used Ingredients Glossary on p.14 or the Index of Recipes on p.143.

Index of Recipes

About The Author

Photograph by Claire Langlois

Aurélie Paré is a self-taught cook who wrote this book (her first) while attending middle school. She has lived in several places in the US and Canada and now resides with her family in Atlantic Canada.

Aurélie pursues a variety of activities including playing the clarinette, sewing, swimming, and walking with her dog. In 2007, she was recognized by Duke TIP.

Now aged 14 years old, she's excited about continuing to cook healthaliciously good food.

She can be contacted by email at:
aurelie@aurelieshealthycuisine.com

Or by mail at:
Aurélie's Healthy Cuisine
860 Mountain Road, Suite 302
Moncton, NB Canada E1C 2N7

Visit her website at:
www.aurelieshealthycuisine.com

Want to have more of *The Healthaliciously Good Cookbook*?

To order additional books, please visit the website address above or send a form including your name, address, telephone number and email address to the address given above along with a payment of 24.95$ Cdn for each book ordered. *Shipping and handling will be billed when order is received.*